Mays, Mantle, Snider

By Donald Honig

Mays, Mantle, Snider

A Celebration

DONALD HONIG

Macmillan Publishing Company

NEW YORK

Collier Macmillan Publishers

LONDON

For my daughter, Cathy

Macmillan Publishing Company
866 Third Avenue, New York, N.Y. 10022
Collier Macmillan Canada, Inc.

Library of Congress Cataloging-in-Publication Data
Honig, Donald.
Mays, Mantle, Snider.
Includes index.
1. Baseball players—United States—Biography.
2. Mays, Willie, 1931–   . 3. Mantle, Mickey,
1931–   . 4. Snider, Duke.   I. Title.
GV865.A1H6192   1987   796.357′092′2 [B]   87-7745
ISBN 0-02-551200-5

Special Sales Director
Macmillan Publishing Company
866 Third Avenue
New York, N.Y. 10022

10 9 8 7 6 5 4 3 2 1

Designed by Nancy Sugihara
Printed in the United States of America

Contents

Acknowledgments

I would like to thank those who gave me the benefit of their good advice and wise counsel during the writing of this book, including Stanley Honig, David Markson, Lawrence Ritter, Thomas Brookman, Allan J. Grotheer, Douglas Mulcahy, Andrew Aronstein, and Louis Kiefer.

A special note of thanks and appreciation to my editor, Jeffrey Neuman, whose vast knowledge of baseball fact and lore was immensely helpful.

Center field. On a baseball diamond, the most commanding and far-reaching assignment. It is an unwritten decree that when the center fielder calls for a ball, all others cease pursuit. "He takes whatever he can get." There is a freebooting sound to that. No other player has so imperative a mandate. He is a player whose boundaries are defined solely by his speed and his daring.

According to one of the game's honored tenets, a team cannot win without being strong "up the middle." That is, there must be players of star caliber catching, at shortstop and second base, and in center field. If a center fielder's résumé doesn't include quick acceleration, speed afoot, a strong throwing arm, unerring judgment of the trajectory of an airborne baseball, and a willingness to gamble that is rooted in good instincts rather than bravado, he had better seek employment elsewhere. While certain heavy hitters of dubious agility afield have been posted at first base or third base or sent to graze in left field, they are never allowed into the center-field pasture.

There is another talent expected of the good center fielder, something that his "up-the-middle" colleagues can survive without—a lively bat. Some of the game's greatest defensive center fielders did hit extremely well, men like Tris Speaker (for years the automatic choice at the position on the all-time team), Edd Roush, and Lloyd Waner; while others of impeccable glove posted acceptable batting averages, like Terry Moore, Dominic DiMaggio, Paul Blair, and Curt Flood. The first center fielder who did everything with extraordinary abundance—fielding with a magnetic glove, running well, firing with a strong and deadly arm, and hitting both for average and with explosive power—was Joe DiMaggio. This remarkable synthesis of talents made DiMaggio unique (and this is not taking into account the array of intangibles that contributed to his uniqueness—his élan on the field, his charisma, and finally his enduring mystique).

So the center fielder who can cover all four points of the outfield compass with dispatch and also possesses a bat that sweeps with the

1

might of a wagon tongue is one of the game's crescendo figures, a rarity among the finest athletes a nation can produce. A star of stars. They appear infrequently, leave behind indelible markings. And yet once, sending the laws of probability into extremes, there were three such performers playing for three different teams in the same city at the same time: Duke Snider of the Brooklyn Dodgers, Mickey Mantle of the New York Yankees, and Willie Mays of the New York Giants. For a time, while they rocketed balls into, and raced to stab them out of, the same municipal sky, they were a litany: Mantle, Mays, and Snider, each the champion of stubbornly opinionated partisans armed with impressive statistics; each a source of deep pride, a bearer of symbolic standards.

Two whites and a black. A left-handed hitter, a switch hitter, a right-handed hitter. A Californian, an Oklahoman, an Alabaman. A Dodger, a Yankee, a Giant. Each a first-magnitude star in years when New York baseball was at its apex—fifteen pennants and eight World Championships in nine years. Three nearly flawless paragons of what the major-

Part of the noise and color of Ebbets Field: the Dodgers "Sym-phony Band." The appreciative music lovers in Brooklyn uniforms are Spider Jorgensen (left) *and Bobby Bragan.*

*A quiet afternoon between the Dodgers and Giants at the Polo Grounds,
September 6, 1953. Furillo and Giants skipper Leo Durocher had words,
then fisticuffs. With the antagonists scuffling somewhere below, the rest of
the boys try to act as peacemakers.*

league center fielder should be. Each a prince carrying the burden of hereditary allegiances, star ballplayers at a time when—in that time and in that city, anyway—a commitment to one of those three teams was an act of utmost loyalty and devotion.

Time in its flight has created insuperable differences between those years and these, and today it is increasingly difficult to explain, and probably more difficult to understand, the fervor of baseball partisanship in the New York of the 1950s. In a city that was less threatened, less pressured, baseball assumed a greater importance, a deeper relevance to its immediate environment, a stronger continuity with a historical past that seemed to mingle palpably with the present.

The scripture was this: No Dodger could ever be better than a Giant, no Giant superior to a Dodger; the Yankees view of their intracity brethren, originating as it did from an unchallenged pinnacle, contained more than a dash of hauteur.

Rooting for—or against—a particular team

Twilight and sunrise: DiMaggio and Mantle in 1951.

was almost a revelation of character and philosophy. It could be cultural (the Dodgers folklore attracted a certain following), or economic (the despised corporate Yankees image), it could be malignantly or benignly racial (the Dodger–Jackie Robinson black revolution), or soberly tradition-bound (Giants fans went back to the turn of the century and John McGraw in their pride). There were lifelong loyalties, inherited as names and blood were inherited, part of one's identity, part of one's neighborhood. There could be shifts of political allegiance, even religious conversion, but who ever heard of a Dodgers fan switching to the Giants?

These three sets of fans were students of one another, and from out of their observations came a self-perpetuating myth. Simply put, the myth was that baseball fans gradually assume the personalities, even the characteristics, of their team. Despite the obviously mythological nature of this notion, it does demonstrate the powerful emotional drawing power of a baseball team, particularly, and perhaps specifically, when one city possesses three teams at the same time. The inevitable rivalries are intense, and from the intensity evolves stereotypes and dubious received wisdom.

Thus the myth of the Yankees fan—supporter of baseball's most successful and affluent franchise—being something of a smug self-congratulator who attended ball games wearing a suit and necktie. This, of course, was the view from "below"—the steerage section of New York City fandom, those glumly resentful partisans of the other two teams. It didn't matter that Yankees fans were drawn from every social and economic distinction; it only mattered that in debate the resources Yankees fans could draw on included Ruth, Gehrig, DiMaggio, all those pennants and World Championships, and that monstrous amphitheater known as the House That Ruth Built, as though it belonged to the same power federation as The House of Morgan and other seats of might and influence.

And the Dodgers fan. Another known quantity (Yankees and Giants fans were certain of this). A rough-hewn, salt-of-the-earth, blue-collar, language-fracturing loudmouth who followed the precepts of an infinite optimism as he rooted doggedly for a band of vivid characters who played in a charming bandbox of surpassing intimacy. The Yankees were the Bronx, while those Dodgers fans derived from a borough that seemed to have been Balkanized; they were Flatbush and Bensonhurst and Brownsville and Bay Ridge and the Gowanus Canal; they filled their beloved little Ebbets Field and rooted fervently for their adored team, beseeching them to do what seemed to come so naturally to those lordly Yankees, whose fans were always so condescending and amused, as at the antics of the rabble.

And Giants fans? Well, the other two looked upon them as dullards who didn't have the sense to opt for power or color. The Giants fans seemed caught in the middle, cold fish dreaming about the days of McGraw, their only apparent emotion one of pure contempt

for their raucous Brooklyn cousins, their only satisfaction coming during those Octobers when the Yankees once again flattened the Dodgers. A Dodgers fan who one day attended a game in the Polo Grounds returned home that evening to report that most of the customers were middle-aged men with vacant smiles. An exaggeration, no doubt, but that was the perception. The Giants were dull, their fans were dull, the Polo Grounds was an atrocity.

For two decades, starting with the turn of the century, New York had been a Giants city, its athletic personality determined and dominated by the arrogant John McGraw and his bruisingly efficient teams, headed by Christy Mathewson. Friend of politicians high and low, of judges and police commissioners and theatrical luminaries, McGraw became part of the city's fabric as no other baseball man, before or since. Neither the Dodgers nor the Yankees could compete with the style or the success of the Giants, "McGraw's Giants," as they were always known—it was like an imprimatur guaranteeing élan and swagger.

But then, shortly after the end of the First World War, McGraw suddenly found himself and his team in a shadow cast dramatically and colossally (and with the theatricality McGraw admired) by the Yankees, or, more specifically, Babe Ruth. Nothing in mankind and few things in nature itself could have competed with that booming slugger and consummate showman. Not only New York but baseball itself became Babe Ruth, a mammoth centrifugal force that roiled the imagination as no other athlete ever had.

In the early 1920s, the Giants won four consecutive pennants and three times locked with Ruth's Yankees in the World Series, in hand-to-hand combat for the championship of the world and of New York. But no matter what they did, the Giants were losing forever their old primacy to the soaring Ruth and the Yankees.

In Brooklyn, there had never been all that

*A panoramic shot of New York baseball: In the foreground is Yankee
Stadium, across the Harlem River the Polo Grounds.*

Duke and Willie: It looks like Willie had the last laugh that day.

much to cheer about. The Dodgers had taken their first pennant in 1916 and their second in 1920, at which time the Giants had won six (and the Yankees none). For the next two decades Dodgers fans had to content themselves with teams of "color," of "characters," teams known in the 1920s as "The Daffy Dodgers," with stories of three men on third base and a bemused manager Wilbert Robinson sitting on the bench with his arms folded wondering at it all; a team that faced bankruptcy in the 1930s; a team that finally became known more for its vociferous and noisily faithful fans than for the nondescript players who passed in and out of its uniform.

With McGraw finally gone in 1932, the Giants continued as a winning team, but one without identifying labels. Bill Terry, their new manager, was humorless and aloof, while star players Mel Ott and Carl Hubbell lacked magnetic force.

While the Giants were performing with quiet efficiency, the Yankees, the post-Ruth Yankees now, were reaching further heights of success with a team built around Joe Di-Maggio in center field, who was setting glamorous new standards for that cynosure position in Yankee Stadium and all through baseball.

After the war, it was Brooklyn that caught

the imagination with the addition to its roster of Jackie Robinson, along with a team of strong, swift, marvelously talented young players signed wholesale during the war by Branch Rickey, operating under his credo that "from out of quantity comes quality."

In Yankee Stadium, DiMaggio was still the center fielder supreme, so sublimely gifted as to appear regal, while in the Polo Grounds the Giants were a power-laden but uninspiring team, failing to contend even as they hit home runs in record numbers.

By 1951, although the Yankees continued to win, the dials and levers of their scintillating center fielder were now going in reverse as discernible rust appeared on the DiMaggio machine. But attendant upon the decline of the great DiMaggio came, with remarkable convergence, the appearance of three young center fielders of astonishing talent who were destined to compete with one another in comparative debates among the city's fans as no other players ever have.

The first of those three sparkling young center fielders to come to New York was Brooklyn's Duke Snider, and there was a certain irony that he came to Ebbets Field and not to Yankee Stadium. He not only covered center field with the immaculate grace of DiMaggio and had the left-handed power swing for which the Stadium was designed, but he also carried an aristocratic nickname that seemed appropriate for a Yankees star in those years of imperial dynasty. Certainly a Duke dispensing his largesse in the blue-collar ambience of Ebbets Field was an anomaly. Nevertheless, he fit in, for like true republicans, those plebeians of the bleachers and grandstands looked upon the Duke as a Dodger, and this conferred its own unique royalty.

In Ebbets Field, everything was singularly defined and highly personal: the fans (reveling in their perceived image), the players, the aura, the traditions to be upheld and perpetuated, the familial intimacy of the ball park itself. It all conspired in the delineation of a truly special baseball team. Even the borough in which it all took place had its own distinct

character. Thanks in large part to Hollywood-bred stereotyping, the borough was known the world over, and when Brooklyn was mentioned the Dodgers were never far behind and invariably referred to in semiliterate stylized Brooklyn "accents." (Even newspaper headlines, in deference to those accents, proclaimed the Dodgers center fielder as "The Dook.") What other fans would have taken pride in having their beloved team known as "Dem Bums"?—a pride that swelled to enormous proportions when the Bums became in the 1950s one of the greatest assemblages in baseball history.

The team had been put together with great skill, each addition like another crisply working spring locking into place: Roy Campanella catching, Gil Hodges at first base, Jackie Robinson at second, Pee Wee Reese at short, Billy Cox at third, Carl Furillo and Duke Snider the outfield core, and Don Newcombe, Preacher Roe, Carl Erskine, and Johnny Podres leading the starting pitching. That they were masterfully joined together by the astute Mr. Rickey is borne out by the fact that once they cohered they continued on with a

Duke Snider with Fort Worth of the Texas League in 1946.

Branch Rickey in 1947.

stability and longevity unusual for a big-league team. Of the above-mentioned, only Roe, Cox, and Robinson were no longer with the team when it left Brooklyn in 1957.

In their decade of glory they won six pennants, plus their memorable 1955 World Series victory. At times they fielded what was virtually an All-Star team. Four of them have been elected to the Hall of Fame—Robinson, Campanella, Reese, and the man who in the opinion of many was the most abundantly gifted of all the Brooklyn Dodgers, center fielder Edwin Donald (Duke) Snider.

Snider was born in the Los Angeles suburb of Compton on September 19, 1926. Compton lies in southern California sunshine country, a veritable greenhouse for the young buds of baseball. One of those buds was Edwin Donald Snider, possessor of athletic ability to burn. For Compton High's baseball team he pitched and batted fourth; for its football team he was a triple-threat tailback, throwing sixty-yard passes and kicking and running; on the basketball team he was high scorer.

This Snider boy, fortunate in so many ways, was also lucky in his parents, a pair of loving and understanding people. Ward Snider, the father, had been a semipro ballplayer back in his native Ohio. The elder Snider had put in a four-year hitch in the United States Navy that ended in 1925, whereupon he settled in California and went to work in the San Diego shipyards as a rigger. His wife, Florence, was herself a transplanted midwesterner, brought to California by her parents from Kansas.

Look at the biographies of most of baseball's top stars, and you see that the father seldom affected a posture of indifference toward the boy's aspirations. There were those fathers who ardently cared about baseball, who with encouragement and coaching tried to cultivate their son's talent and ambition. And there were those who were downright hostile toward their son's interest in the game, who considered the time spent playing it wasted. Ward Snider was of the former mold. Maybe the onetime Ohio semipro was trying to exorcise the ghosts of old frustrations and disappointments—not an uncommon story if he was—but it doesn't matter. What matters is his son grew up to be a stellar center fielder, a star in New York City, a World Series hero, a Hall of Famer.

Ward Snider wanted his son, his only child, to play baseball, and when the boy was seven years old there were already enough manifestations of real talent and desire to quicken an old ballplayer's pulse. The father's approach to baseball was serious and businesslike. He himself had been gifted enough to know that if you could play this game well, then this was the way you were going to play it or not at all. You were going to learn to play it correctly, because baseball was more than merely hitting and catching and throwing; there were all of those subtle mechanisms and nuances to learn and master that enabled you to hone your abilities to the point where they were at all times poised on automatic.

"It wasn't always easy," Ward Snider recalled years later. "Once I had to whack his butt. But it helped cure him of the habit of backing up on fly balls and ground balls, which gives the runner a needless advantage." (Most boys run the risk of corporal punishment through truancy or some other mischief; young Duke Snider faced it for backing up on a fly ball.) Another thing Ward Snider taught his boy was "to catch a ball above his shoulder, and be ready for a throw."

That last bit of learning might evoke nostalgic gleams in the memories of old Dodgers fans of the Duke gliding across the green surface of Ebbets Field and taking a ball eye-

Ebbets Field.

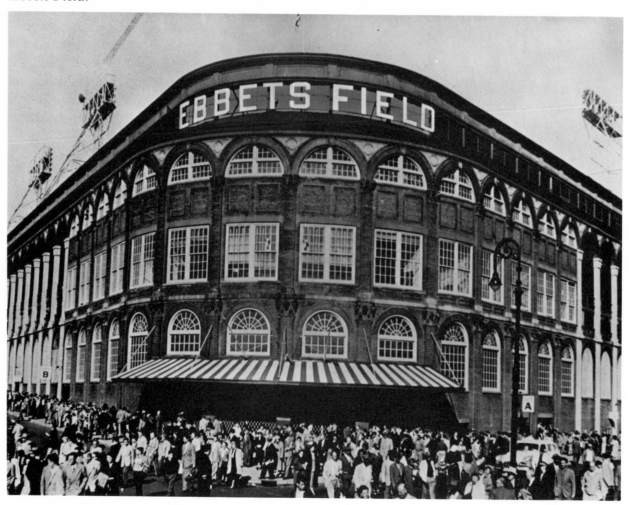

high or shoulder-high, in the DiMaggio style.

It was Ward Snider who turned his naturally right-handed son into a lefty. "His reasoning was simple," Duke said. "He kept telling me there was a gold mine in baseball for left-handed hitters. Most of the pitchers were right-handed, the ballparks were built for left-handers, and you had a two-step advantage going to first base." Here was a grown man talking hardheaded baseball logic to a boy of six or seven years old. You can almost see the father savoring the dream.

Ironically, it was the young Duke's pitching that first attracted the big-league scouts—a no-hitter Snider fired against Beverly Hills High. The scouts came for a readout on a young pitcher, but then they saw him swing a bat and throw and field—he was seventeen now and so alive with talent that those Geiger counters scouts carry between their ears must have been chattering—and when they saw all that, they forgot about a pitcher. But they also had to forget, for the time being, about signing the boy; Snider was still in high school and therefore out of bounds to professional baseball. Nevertheless, several of the scouts made sure to stop by the Snider home to make their names and their interest known to young Duke and his mother—Ward Snider had reentered the navy and was off somewhere in the Pacific.

This was 1944 now, the third year of America at war, and professional baseball was at its nadir. The armed services had drained the big-league rosters, and there just wasn't enough talent to go around, from the majors on down. Hunting for big-league ivory was depressing; but for the scouts in Compton the

Rookie Duke Snider sitting on the bench (left) *while Brooklyn's starting infield has its picture taken, early in the 1947 season* (left to right)*: third baseman Spider Jorgensen, shortstop Pee Wee Reese, second baseman Ed Stanky, first baseman Jackie Robinson.*

A trim young Snider in the early 1950s.

There was no big money then, no hefty bonuses. There was only opportunity, and how persuasive a scout could be. And in those years no scouts were more persuasive—or persistent—than those in the employ of the Brooklyn Dodgers, men who had been instructed and lectured at the frothiest font in baseball by the game's most hypnotic evangelist. Branch Rickey's message was plain enough: Get out there and sign every boy who shows the merest spark of talent, and when this war ends we're going to be ahead of everybody else, we're going to be in the midst of building the finest farm system in baseball: not starting to, but in the midst of.

So it was a very positive pitch those Dodgers scouts were making to gifted teenagers and their parents around the country in 1944. They were selling an organization that was looking ahead, that promised the finest building and development program for young ballplayers that existed anywhere on God's green earth. With all of the minor-league teams the Dodgers owned and would own, there would be a place and an opportunity for a boy to show what he could do.

That message must have sounded rich and evocative in those grim years, and that was how the Dodgers signed youngsters like Ralph Branca, Carl Erskine, Rex Barney, Gil Hodges, and many others, including Edwin Donald Snider, who preferred to be known as "Duke," a name pinned on him by a proud father when the boy was five years old, a nickname itself redolent of the times when the Hollywood screen resonated with names like "Ace" and "Lucky."

Snider had received scholarship offers from several schools, including UCLA and USC, but the youngster knew that before long he would be joining his father in the navy and wanted to experience professional baseball before he left.

The letters Snider had written produced only one respondent—Tom Downey of the Brooklyn Dodgers, who came offering a $750 cash bonus if the boy would sign a contract with

sight of this boy must have been like a sudden and startling reaffirmation of all that they held dear.

When Snider graduated high school, he wrote letters to the Dodgers and to the other clubs that had contacted him, letting them know he was available and asking if they were still interested. He didn't know that the Dodgers sleuths had been watching him for a year and compiling a dossier. (As early as the summer of 1943, when he was just sixteen, the Dodgers had invited him to a tryout camp at Long Beach where he had widened the eyes of Branch Rickey, Jr. "You could see it right then and there," the younger Rickey said. "All of it. All of what he was going to become.")

Roy Campanella, Dodgers catcher and three-time National League Most Valuable Player.

Brooklyn's Montreal farm club that called for a salary of $275 per month.

With his father away, the decision was left to Duke's mother. Hoping that she was doing the right thing, she gave her permission and the contract was signed. Actually, it was probably the same decision Ward Snider would have made, since the Sniders had on their hands a youngster who was already a Dodgers fan, having been thus indoctrinated by enchantment with the 1941 team, the brawling, colorful pennant winners, the greatest of Dodgers teams until the ones starring the Duke came along a decade later. If a boy was going to root for a baseball team that was three thousand miles from his home, that team, by all that was logical, should have been the New York Yankees; but perhaps it was some sort of prescience that made players like Pee Wee Reese and Pete Reiser—future teammates—more appealing to him than the likes of Joe DiMaggio and Phil Rizzuto. He had

listened to radio broadcasts of the 1941 World Series between the Dodgers and the Yankees, and maybe it was the raucous chords of Ebbets Field as they sounded upon the mild unoffending climes of Compton three thousand miles away; maybe it all sounded too exotic to be ignored. But whatever cast the spell, the dream was to play in Brooklyn, a place he had never seen, for a team that never came within two thousand miles of him. Baseball, in the pretelevision years, could weave inexplicable enchantments.

In late February 1944, Snider boarded a train in Los Angeles and set out on the long transcontinental ride to the Dodgers spring training camp (reversing the geographical direction of America's traditional pursuit of fame and glory). Because of wartime travel restrictions, the Dodgers, along with the other major-league teams, had not traveled to their usual spring camps in the sunshine but instead were stretching their muscles into shape near to home, in the less hospitable northern climate.

The Dodgers pitched their camp at Bear Mountain, a few miles down the road from the United States Military Academy at West Point, whose facilities had been made available to the ball club. It was a spring training camp with snow (which Snider had never seen before) and with winter winds that roared down from the mountain and up from the river ("I didn't even own an overcoat," Snider said. "I'd never heard of them."). Another force of nature that was new to the seventeen-year-old Californian was named Leo Durocher, Brooklyn's astute, noisily self-confident manager, who dealt with equal flair with coaches, players, and the hard-bitten New York sportswriters—a brigade of them in those days when the city had ten or a dozen dailies. And even though most bona fide big leaguers were serving in the armed forces, Snider still found himself on the same field with some genuine

Right fielder Carl Furillo: He hit line drives and, with the strongest arm in the league, threw them, too.

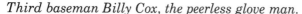

Third baseman Billy Cox, the peerless glove man.

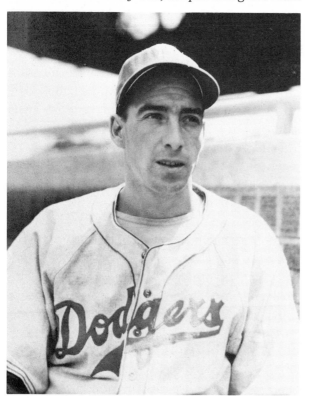

talent—veterans like Dixie Walker, Augie Galan, Paul Waner, Whitlow Wyatt, and Mickey Owen.

It was quite a breaking-in process for a youngster away from home—a continent away—for the first time, coming all the way from a land of fair weather to take spring training in a cold, snow-whipped place called Bear Mountain. He may have been the best ballplayer and all-around athlete in Compton scholastic circles, but now he was surrounded by a lot of other kids who had been the best in their part of the country too, in their school, town, county, state; not to mention Dixie Walker and Paul Waner and the others who had been going through the big-league grinder for years and years. The Duke was cold and he was lonely and he was homesick; but one thing he was not—intimidated. Not only did he have plenty of talent, he also had a stubborn belief in it and a very fixed opinion about how it should best be employed. And right

The Duke bringing home the bacon, with son Kevin waiting to see what's in the bag.

there was the Duke Snider of the glorious Ebbets Field future—a sumptuously gifted baseball player of limitless potential, and a personality that didn't mind sulking and brooding when things didn't go quite right.

The talent showed before the temperament (and a good thing, too; the other way around would have been risky). The team was holding practice sessions at the Field House at West Point, waiting for the weather to become a bit more accommodating. In early April, with the winds easing and the temperature moderating, the team moved out into the crisp sunshine for a game against the army team. In the lineup for a look-see, Snider caught Rickey's attention by hammering a tremendous home run over the right fielder's head.

Later, Rickey was talking to the writers. "Did you see that boy's power?" the boss said. "And did you see him run, and did you see him throw? He has steel springs in his legs." It made for very good copy. Power. Speed. Strength. *Steel springs*. And the frequently effusive Mr. Rickey wasn't just painting the air; the writers had seen it for themselves. Everyone liked the way this handsome boy with the bright smile looked out there.

That was the talent, and the interest generated by its potential. But even from the beginning, the temperament was companion to it. The Duke's singular disposition was not a product of the big-league swells but part of the first bag he packed. Maybe it was understandable. Here was a boy, and then a man,

Pete Reiser: A world of talent, but not an ounce of luck.

who had everything: the almost unflawed physical ability; the rangy, perfectly proportioned physique; the fresh-minted California good looks, made brighter still by that ingratiating smile. But the man who has everything often has low tolerance for the snags and thorns of life, and frustration and impatience come easily. In Snider's case it wasn't just left-handed pitching that clouded his sunny days; it could be some picayune mal-

function of the world's. Like the time the team arrived at a hotel early one morning and found the rooms were not quite ready; the Duke reportedly fumed aloud with words sulphurous enough to make the lobby's potted plants blush. There were those who maintained that if Snider made out in his first time at bat, that initial frustration was enough to cut back his game for the remaining innings, whereas if he hit safely the first time up, it put him

A smiling Snider touching home plate after clouting a grand-slam homer.
The welcome home committee includes Reese (1), Campanella (39), and Hodges.

in the mood to tear apart the game single-handedly.

The fledgling Duke was not only unused to playing baseball at the base of a stone-cold mountain slope; he was also unused to the regimen of a big-league training camp, much less one overseen by the professionally fastidious Mr. Rickey. Snider was a normal, healthy seventeen-year-old, an age when you have to work to get out of shape rather than the other way around. For this teenager, as for any other, baseball meant going out there and whacking the ball and catching it, not doing wind sprints and calisthenics. He found the whole training routine boring and re-

sponded to it by brooding and sulking. This would, and did, catch the Rickey eye as surely as the boy's wondrous talent had. Rickey pondered the situation, weighed and measured his man, and then told Master Snider to turn in his uniform and leave the camp.

Rickey, of course, had no intention of casting out this rough-edged gem. Snider was simply receiving a serving of what ballplayers large and small had been getting for thirty years—the Rickey treatment, which came in all forms, shades, and varieties. And no one received more calculated and purposeful attention than those of whom Rickey suspected future greatness. As much as on his judicious

Jackie Robinson.

eye for talent, Rickey prided himself upon his knowledge of human nature (which he proved supremely in his selection of Jackie Robinson to break the color barrier in organized baseball). Each of these large-sized talents called for special handling. Order a Dizzy Dean from a camp, and you would have received a horse-laugh; order a Joe Medwick to turn in his uniform, and you ran the risk of seeing that brooding mass of muscles cut a trail, probably after punching somebody in the nose. Rickey had learned to live with the high jinks of Dean and the surliness of Medwick because those boys could light up a ball field. (In the professions, the level of tolerance is adjusted by the sum of the talent.)

If young Snider had known the esteem in which the Dodgers held him, he could have told Rickey to put it in his hat and punch it, and the Old Man would have worn it. But with Snider, Rickey's ploy worked. The young Duke was a clean-living, likable boy nurturing that dream to play for the Brooklyn Dodgers. He went to Rickey's son, Branch Jr., apologized, asked for another chance, and promised to hustle and do whatever the club asked of him.

"Sure, we bluffed him," the younger Rickey said years later. "He was just a kid, and while he had a lot of self-confidence, he still didn't realize how good he was. Let Duke Snider walk out of your camp? We would have hired cops to stop him."

The Dodgers sent the youngster to Newport

News, Virginia, in the Class B Piedmont League. Riding the buses to Richmond and Roanoke and Lynchburg during the days and nights of that wartime summer, Snider batted .294 and led the league with 34 doubles, a modest nine home runs, and an eye-catching 25 assists. With this confidence-builder of a season tucked away, Snider signed up and spent the 1945 season in the navy.

Many ballplayers emerged from military service with damaged or tarnished skills that no amount of work could restore. Some of them were young, some were old; some suffered from combat experience, while others simply slowed or aged and left it somewhere. A cold breeze on a warm arm, a snag in the coordination or the merest blunting of a reflex, and you became a water tank watching streamliners. Washington's fine shortstop Cecil Travis endured frozen feet during the Battle of the Bulge, and when he returned, "I was still a perfectly normal man; I just wasn't a big leaguer anymore. Didn't have that mobility." The Cardinals right-hander Johnny Beazley,

Robinson has just fed to Reese, who is attempting a midair completion of a double play. The man in the dust is Boston's Tommy Holmes.

a 21-game-winning rookie in 1942, pitched for his service club with an out-of-shape arm in 1944 because he "didn't want to let the guys down" and lost it all that day. There were others.

So the clubs held their breath and crossed their fingers and waited for their players to come home, to see what two or three or four years away had done to the tension in those delicately balanced skills.

The Dodgers soon found out about the boy from Compton. Snider was released from the navy after the 1946 season had begun. While waiting to be assigned to a club in the Dodgers vast minor-league network, he attended a Brooklyn tryout camp in San Diego, figuring to put in a little work.

Those mass tryout camps are pretty much a thing of the past now, but at one time they were commonplace events around the country. The big-league clubs held them periodically, and the gate was wide open. Word flew around the city or the countryside or wherever the tryouts were being held, and every youngster with a dream, a glove, and a pair of spikes showed up. There might be hundreds of them, tall and short, round and slim, talented and not. They came to that community field, or that high school diamond, or that minor-league ball park, and everyone received at least one round of equal opportunity. (And for many youngsters attending the Dodger tryout camps in the immediate postwar years, seeing black aspirants showing up and expanding the furthest ripples of the Jackie Robinson revolution was an enlightening experience.) They wore their team uniforms, or parts of uniforms, or sometimes just undershirts and work trousers, and maybe not even spikes but sneakers or scuffed shoes. But whatever, there they were, all equal in the range and purity of their dream. Overseeing it all were two or three scouts, seldom more; men in their forties or fifties and sometimes older, wearing the team colors, real big-league uniforms, those magical, achingly familiar uniforms which more than anything

Duke Snider.

else were the sanction of the occasion. These regents strode about in the hot sun with their clipboards, their air of authority tinged with impatience because they had been doing this long enough to know what the percentages were, that out of the hundreds of youngsters with flapping paper numbers pinned to their backs they would be lucky to find two or three boys good enough to warrant an invitation to come back tomorrow.

When they lined up the outfielders on this hot day in San Diego the boys were some 350 feet from home plate. They were going to have to make that throw, there and then, and it was a brutally telling exercise, because unless it is hurting, your arm, unlike your bat or glove, is not going to have a bad day. Your arm was what it was, crafted and muscled by nature, and it wasn't going to get much better, and with one or two throws you had told those scouts in those beckoning uniforms all they needed to know about it.

Arthur Dede, a Dodgers scout who was not in San Diego that day but heard the story,

Snider about to hit the dirt after going from first to third on a Jackie Robinson single; awaiting the throw, Braves third baseman Bob Elliott. The Duke was safe. It happened at Ebbets Field, May 1949.

told it a few years later when Snider had become the Duke of Flatbush.

"The scouts knew who he was, of course, so they let him unwind first. The distance was around 350 feet, maybe a little more. He took the ball and fired it in on a line, right into the catcher's glove without a bounce. There were about forty or fifty other kids waiting to throw, and when they saw that, none of them wanted to be next. Each one said he had to warm up a little more, that he wasn't ready."

What those other boys had seen, what they had experienced, was a moment of truth at once jarring and sobering. A flash of big-league magic.

"And then they ran them," Dede said. "A

sixty-yard dash." Not in competition with one another, but against a stopwatch. Once again "the kid with the arm" showed them what they were up against, what it was all about. He ran it in 6.7—the world record at the time for a man in a track suit and sneakers was 6.1.

And then when those aspirants saw that same kid come to bat and hoist several long, towering drives into the distance, they knew they were seeing the dream they had dreamed for themselves.

This was a plum nearing full ripeness, ready for swifter competition. Rickey decided to send Snider (already hailed by one Dodgers scout as "another Ted Williams") to Fort Worth of the Texas League, a high-caliber Double-A circuit. The young man got into 68 games, batted .250, hit five home runs. Hardly anything out of the ordinary there, except further evidence that statistics often keep their own counsel. A .250 batting average tells you nothing about the ferocious snap in the boy's swing, and buried in the modest five home runs is the telltale power of one of them. (Fortuitously witnessed by Mr. Rickey himself, it is said.) In July, Snider launched a shot that witnesses swore was preparing to leave the county when last seen (anywhere else but Texas, and they might have said it was leaving the state). It soared over a clock mounted atop the right-center-field fence, a distance of 430 feet, and disappeared. A .250 batting average and five home runs? Forget them. Statistics can be like opinions—only as informed or as interesting as the person spouting them. As far as the Dodgers were concerned, Duke Snider was as good as a certified check.

Twenty years old, with just one-and-a-half seasons of professional ball behind him, Snider went to spring training with the Dodgers in 1947. When the writers gathered at the team's training camp—in Havana that year— they heard Rickey pronounce the young man "the jewel of the organization." This conferred distinction was no small potatoes; at the time the Dodgers had a farm system brimming, and in places overstocked, with gifted youngsters playing for twenty-six farm clubs, from Pueblo, Colorado, to Mobile, Alabama; from Nashua, New Hampshire, to Sheboygan, Wisconsin; from Montreal, Canada, to Valdosta, Georgia. The boy had a "perfect" swing, a powerful arm, and those legs that the Old Man never tired of calling "steel springs" ("The most famous legs since Betty Grable's," one jaded writer finally muttered), and was potentially "another Musial," which in 1947 was as gaudy a prophecy as could be made.

Another Musial. Naturally. No gifted rookie is ever himself in a spring camp, nor can he be, since he has developed no persona yet, and

so in order to establish a reference point he is inevitably compared to someone else. This kind of trumpeting is the stuff of spring training camps, just the sort of copy needed to warm up the hometown folk shivering in the March winds. Spring training hyperbole seems almost a thing of the past now, as though it were synonymous with an old, ingenuous optimism. Maybe it was the competition among the dozen or so New York dailies, each needing a story each day; maybe the writers were more credulous or more accommodating as flacks for the club; or maybe it's simply that today a player that good would have been brought up in midseason the year before. When Mickey Mantle showed up in the Yankees spring camp in 1951 he was virtually unknown, having spent the previous season in Class C ball. But his stunning abilities impressed everyone from Casey Stengel right on through the New York press corps. Taking their lead from Stengel, the writers began firing dispatches back to New York that fairly quivered with superlatives, to the extent that

Snider is out at first in the second game of the 1949 World Series at Yankee Stadium. The first baseman is Tommy Henrich.

Stengel, who had preferred at least another year of seasoning for Mantle, told the writers, "Because of you guys I've got to bring him in with me. New York wants to see him." By the time he reached New York that April, Mantle's arrival had created terrific anticipation, and when he didn't immediately fulfill expectations, the advance publicity proved to have been harmful.

Though his advance notices were lavish, Snider's buildup was not as excessive as that given Mantle four years later. One reason was the Dodgers had something else cooking that spring, a story even bigger than the hatching of "another Musial." In the opinion of one writer, while Rickey genuinely believed in Snider's potential for stardom, the Old Man was also hoping to create some puff as a diversionary tactic, "trying to get the boys to perhaps look away from what was the big story in 1947." That story was the first black player trying to make a major-league team. The story was Jackie Robinson. Were the Dodgers going to promote him to the big team's roster, and if so, when? Rickey was being purposefully coy, playing out his game in his own way, in his own time. He wanted as little focus on Jackie as possible. The team was training in Havana expressly because of Robinson, to keep him away from Florida's barbaric Jim Crow laws, free of taunts and threats. Jackie was in fact not even training with the Dodgers but with the Montreal Royals at another facility some miles away.

So it was a far from normal spring training experience for the Brooklyn Dodgers in 1947. Many of those young athletes were being compelled to break into the big leagues—a tough enough endeavor at any time—under the conditions of pending social revolution. Many who became the stalwarts of those superb teams of the fifties were being treated to a deeper and more complex view of the world and of human nature than any young ballplayers before or since. Carl Furillo, Gil Hodges, Duke Snider, Carl Erskine, Ralph Branca, and others were young men trying

First baseman Gil Hodges: Check those muscles.

to mold big-league careers when Robinson was beginning to bring democracy to major-league baseball. None of these men were particularly naive—some were combat veterans—but the invective and humiliation endured by Robinson shocked and offended them, including some of the team's southern players, not partial to Robinson to begin with. Reality descended all around the Brooklyn Dodgers that spring and summer, convulsing the supposedly sacrosanct, above-the-fray atmosphere of major-league ball. It came from the newspapers, grandstands, opposing dugouts, and even, for a time, from their own clubhouse. Rickey's "cause," "movement," "experiment"—it had many appellations—was part of baseball and at the same time a transcending force. It couldn't have been pleasant watching a teammate go through that crucible day after day no matter what your initial predisposition; it was tough enough to go into the hinterlands representing a New York City club without also arousing the venom of racists.

"The experience affected us, whether we realized it at the time or not," Gil Hodges recalled in later years. "We couldn't help but to see what Jackie was going through. I know it bothered a lot of the guys, and while we still had a lot of fun on those clubs, we knew we were seeing a more serious side of things. I think it toughened us, helped us to appreciate one another as human beings a little more and draw us closer together as a team. There was a lot of mutual understanding, a lot of togetherness on those teams."

Snider made the team that spring and went north with the Dodgers—to sit on the bench. Brooklyn's regular outfield had Gene Hermanski and Carl Furillo platooning in left

Shortstop Pee Wee Reese, captain of the great Dodgers teams of the 1950s.

field, Pete Reiser in center, and Dixie Walker in right. There was no outcry from press or fans on behalf of the "new Musial." Robinson, promoted to the Dodgers just before opening day, was the story, riveting all attention.

Through the first forty or so games of the season, Snider was strictly a pinch hitter and occasional late-inning outfield replacement. The Hermanski-Furillo tandem was doing well in left field, Walker was a fixture in right, and center field belonged to Reiser.

Pistol Pete had come to the Dodgers in 1940 and a year later was a twenty-two-year-old batting champion, the most exciting young player in the National League, described by Branch Rickey as "the greatest natural talent I have ever seen." Years later when Leo Durocher called Willie Mays the greatest young ballplayer *he* had ever seen, he qualified it by adding that Pete Reiser had been every bit as good and might even have been better.

A series of injuries had decreased Reiser's efficiency, however, and his once-matchless talents were in deterioration; but even though the now twenty-eight-year-old center fielder was no longer the player he had been, he was still a throbbing presence in the Brooklyn outfield, a daredevil—some said reckless— player, both afield and on the bases.

On the night of June 4, 1947, at Ebbets Field, Reiser turned in center field to pursue a long fly ball off the bat of Pittsburgh's Cully Rikard. The ball carried, and Reiser never took his eye off it, running at top speed toward the solid concrete wall. He caught the ball just before smashing into the wall. The impact was brutal.

Reiser was carried off the field; his replacement, making his first appearance as Brooklyn's center fielder, was rookie Duke Snider. A few days later, on June 6, Snider made his first start in center. The club had decided to give him a shot. He hit tolerably well over the next few weeks, but not well enough for a center fielder on a club fighting for a pennant, not with Furillo there and with Reiser coming back.

This superb Dodgers outfield was together for two years, 1951–52 (left to right): *Furillo, Snider, and Andy Pafko.*

In midseason, batting .258 with no home runs, Snider was sent to St. Paul of the American Association, where the Dodgers wanted him to play regularly.

He hadn't played much in Brooklyn, but enough to leave behind a clear imprint of the Snider personality. He had manifested a low tolerance for frustration and a penchant for demonstrating his displeasure with himself. If he had a poor day at the plate, he was apt to throw bats, kick water coolers, and remodel some clubhouse furniture. And sulk.

"He was temperamental as hell," one teammate recalled. "He hated to strike out. I mean, really *hated* it. You could see the smoke come out of his ears. There was no question he had

the ability, but you can never be sure if a guy's going to put it together. Ability by itself is no guarantee. You've got to have self-discipline."

Things were a little easier at St. Paul. In 66 games, Snider batted .316 and tagged 12 home runs. In the spring of 1948, he was back in the Dodgers camp, in the Dominican Republic that year. Still not totally conversant with the strike zone, he was sent by Rickey to Vero Beach, Florida, for a more intensive education. There he saw another struggling Dodger, Pete Reiser. Knowing that Snider was going to blossom at any moment, and preferring not to risk exposing Reiser to outfield walls anymore, the Dodgers had their one-

Manager Charlie Dressen and his ace right-hander Don Newcombe. That horseshoe worked wonders for Newk in 1955–56, when he won 47 and lost just 12.

Sinkerballing relief ace Clem Labine.

time brilliant center fielder working out at first base. The transition was not going well. His long history of injuries had mortally damaged Reiser's abilities; the glittering edge of his running speed was gone; and his heart was not in the first-base experiment. At twenty-nine he was an old man.

For Snider, watching Pete Reiser—one of his heroes on the 1941 Dodgers team—struggle on a ball field was a sobering experience. It was also a cautionary one. Snider resolved that spring not to fall victim to a Reiser syndrome, to always be thinking when racing back for a fly ball, to know at all times just where he was in relation to the wall and how rapidly the distance was narrowing. It was a lesson the intuitive young ballplayer learned well, for throughout the years he played center field in Ebbets Field's neighborly boundaries, he never did injure himself running into a wall; instead he made leaping, perfectly timed catches of spectacular grace, in part a legacy bequeathed the Dodgers by the luckless Pete Reiser.

Duke Snider.

But Snider's primary task was learning the strike zone. Rickey had the young man stand at home plate, bat on shoulder, being pitched to but not allowed to swing. It was Duke's job to call each pitch, a ball or strike, and then turn around to see how his judgment corresponded with that of the coach who was playing umpire. He was taught to lay off the tempting high fastball and ignore the teasers that broke into the dirt. Gradually he learned the zone wherein the hitter made a living, not the pitcher.

Snider began the 1948 season in Montreal. As soon as his record merited it, Rickey told him, the Duke would be back. By midseason the record merited it: 77 games, 77 runs batted in, 17 home runs, a .327 batting average. He finished the season with Brooklyn, back to stay now, getting into 53 games, hitting five home runs, batting just .244. But like the Fort Worth statistics, the Brooklyn numbers were meaningless. The Dodgers liked what they saw. Their center fielder had arrived.

He was a regular on the 1949 club, experiencing the excitement and exhilaration of a tension-wracked pennant race that would not be settled until the tenth inning of the season's final game. His first full season was a splendid one—23 home runs, 92 runs batted in, .292 batting average, and in addition covering center field as well as Reiser ever had.

But the Dodgers organization was still waiting for Snider to mature. This no longer meant keeping his awesome power swing in the strike zone. The club was waiting for him to curb his outbursts, such as showing graphic displeasure at being struck out, brooding when in a slump, speaking intemperately to writers (with whom he was never to feel totally comfortable). It was all part of a single package, going back to all of that athletic brilliance on the playing fields of Compton, where nothing had been able to withstand the onslaught of Duke Snider. That old dominance and the triumphs and expectations it had bred were now in the big leagues, contending with all of those other boys, the heroes of a hundred Comptons, to whom Duke Snider was indeed a threat but one whom they reckoned to handle. After all, those boys were also dealing with Stan Musial, Jackie Robinson, Ralph Kiner, Johnny Mize, and the rest of the thunderbolts.

The Duke could explode, he could pout, he could sulk. And then he could feel contrite about it. But not always. There are times when an athlete's talent—wrapped so tightly with ego and passion—simply will not allow itself to be humbled. Like the time when Dodgers manager Burt Shotton ordered the Duke (batting around .330 at the moment) to bunt with two men on and none out. The young slugger didn't like it, and liked it even less when he bunted a pop-up for an easy out. He returned to the bench smoldering, and before he sat down said, loud enough for all to hear, "What kind of baseball is it when a .330 hitter is told to bunt?"

Shotton, a reserved gentleman, sidled a glance but said nothing. After the game, how-

Ballet, baseball-style, Ebbets Field, August 1949: Snider (top), Robinson, and Furillo converge on a fly ball, with Furillo making the grab (note the ball in the webbing of his glove). Umpire Jocko Conlan's right in the spirit of things.

ever, he ordered a one-hundred-dollar fine levied against Snider, to be remitted if the Duke would offer an apology in front of the club. The young man refused. He would pay the fine.

"I'm not sure, but I think I admired him for it," a reflective Shotton said a few years later. "It cost him, but he stuck to his guns. And who knows? Maybe the boy was right. Maybe you shouldn't ask a .330 hitter to bunt."

The Dodgers had to win the last game of the 1949 season to clinch the pennant. Play-ing the Phillies in Philadelphia, they dissi-pated an early 5–0 lead, struggled back and forth, and went into the top of the tenth in-ning snagged in a 7–7 tie. Reese led off with a single, was sacrificed to second and scored on Duke Snider's clutch, game-winning, pen-nant-winning single, a hit that propelled the Dodgers into the World Series against the Yankees, who had also clinched in a close game on the same day. There had never been a day like it in the history of New York base-ball—two of the city's teams fighting for their

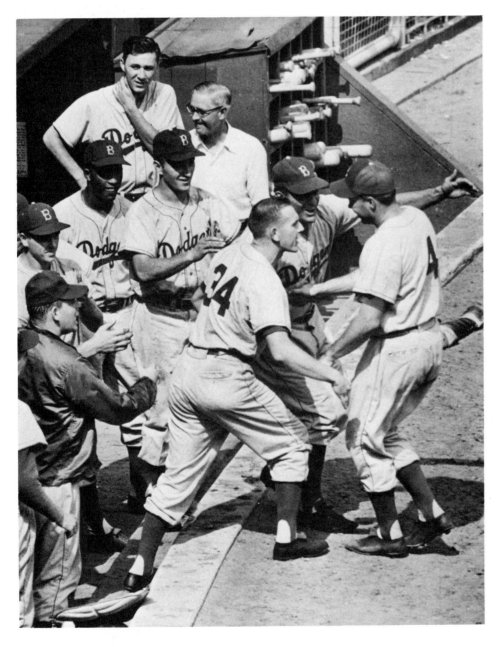

The Duke receiving an enthusiastic reception after belting one out.

Joe Black, hard-throwing relief pitcher whose outstanding work in 1952 helped the Dodgers win the pennant.

league's championship on the final day, and both winning. (Given the precepts of New York baseball, however, the only people celebrating both victories were the kind who called New York "Our Town," like politicians and newspaper editorialists.)

There was no occasion more riveting for the city than an all–New York World Series, and at that particular time it was more publicly encompassing and involving than before or since. In those years, before the proliferation of television sets in every home, people gathered in bars to watch the games; also, appliance stores set up receivers in their windows, both as goodwill gesture and merchandising device, attracting crowds of passersby who lingered on the sidewalk in front of the store to watch a pitch, an at bat, an inning or more, creating vocal knots of witnesses all around the city, making the Series a more intimate public event than ever before.

For Duke Snider, playing in a World Series had been his "biggest and most important dream" (there's a real American kid talking), and he pressed hard. Too hard, probably. Enough to have him describe the 1949 Series as the greatest disappointment of his life (this

was before Bobby Thomson's big pop in 1951). As the Yankees rolled across the Dodgers in five games, Snider batted just .143 and set a doleful (five-game) record by striking out eight times.

But bad Series or not, the Yankees had taken note of him. The strikeouts notwithstanding, the savage fluidity of that swing had made an impression. "He has terrific ability," Joe DiMaggio said. "He struck out a lot because he was trying to kill the ball. With all his natural power, he could take plenty off his swing and still hit it out of the park." Nor had Snider's brilliant defensive play gone unnoticed. "He's as good as anybody out there," said Stengel, whose own man out there was the still peerless DiMaggio.

The last game of the 1950 season was an uncanny replay of the year before. Again the Dodgers were playing the Phillies, and again the pennant was afloat, waiting to be seized. The difference this time was that the Dodgers

Right-hander Carl Erskine.

Snider at the batting cage in Vero Beach, Florida.

were one game behind the team they were playing and needed a win to force a playoff. With the score tied 1–1 in the bottom of the ninth, Snider lined a sharp single to center that sent the winning run home from second base; but this time the runner, Cal Abrams, didn't make it. He was thrown out at home. The Phillies held on and won the game—and the pennant—in the top of the tenth. Snider's single and the putout at home became part of Brooklyn lore, on the melancholy side, along with Mickey Owen's dropped third strike, Pete Reiser's injuries, Bobby Thomson's home run, and Don Larsen's perfect game.

Brooklyn's center fielder, however, could take satisfaction in having made a surge to full-fledged stardom in 1950. The clutch single in the final game had been his 199th hit, good enough to lead the league. He hit 31 home runs, drove in 107 runs, batted .321, and of course played center field with unerring sureness. All of the forecasts that had been made about the young man were being borne out.

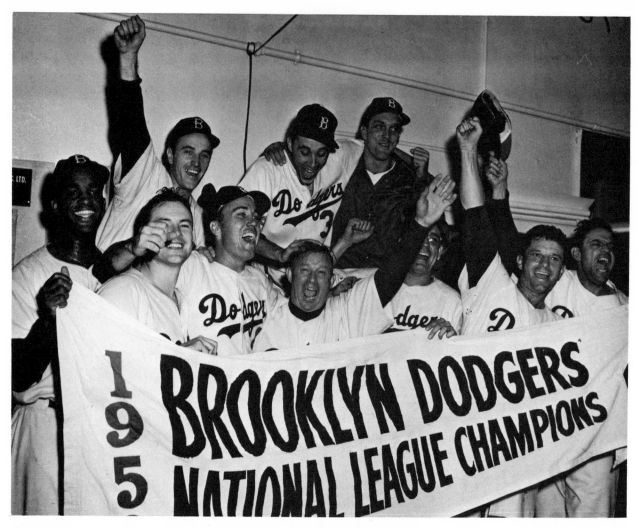

A jubilant group of Brooklyn Dodgers celebrating their 1952 pennant-clinching:
(front row, left to right) *Joe Black, pitcher Johnny Rutherford, Snider, Charlie Dressen, pitcher Clyde King, Andy Pafko, coach Cookie Lavagetto;* (back, left to right) *outfielder George Shuba, pitcher Billy Loes, Carl Erskine.*

In 1951, the Dodgers again lost the pennant in their final game, this time to Bobby Thomson's home run. Though Snider hit 29 home runs and drove in 101 runs, his hitting tailed off during the September stretch run, and he finished up at .277. It was the year that Mays and Mantle came to New York, Willie an immediate success in center for the Giants, Mickey going to right field for the Yankees as DiMaggio played out his final season. The compelling three-way rivalry was not quite ready to begin, however. Mays was drafted into the army early in the 1952 season, and

Mantle was still several years away from stardom.

Though young Mantle had respectable seasons in 1952 and 1953, his efforts were going unappreciated by some highly vocal segments in Yankee Stadium, who were booing Mickey for the quaint reason that he was not Joe DiMaggio. So for those seasons, New York's unchallenged center fielder was Brooklyn's Snider.

In 1952, Snider dropped to 21 home runs and 92 runs batted in, but raised his average to .303 as the Dodgers won the pennant. From mid-August to the end of the season he blistered the ball at a near-.400 clip. According to some people, there was a story behind this surge, one that had made Snider a highly motivated man. When he began his surge, he was hitting around .280, far below what the club expected of him. With the Dodgers locked in another pennant race with the Giants, manager Charlie Dressen abruptly benched his center fielder in a game against Philadelphia's southpaw ace Curt Simmons. A day or so later, Mike Gaven of the New York *Journal-American* wrote the following:

Charlie Dressen has made the most important decision of his managerial career. He has decided to bench Duke Snider, often called baseball's greatest potential star. . . . Obviously the ulterior motive is to light a fire under the speedy and hard-hitting 26-year-old outfielder and remind him that he must supplement his great natural talent with more effort.

By the same token he is reminded, and obviously with Walter O'Malley's consent, that he is subjecting himself to a 25% cut in salary unless his play improves when and if he returns to regular duty.

Furillo (left) *and Snider have Ted Williams surrounded before a spring training game.*

The Dodgers line up in batting order before the start of the 1952 World Series (left to right): *Cox, Reese, Snider, Robinson, Campanella, Pafko, Hodges, Furillo, Black. Place hitters seven and eight tell you the kind of lineup this was.*

Dressen's drastic move also tells other clubs that Snider . . . probably will be on the market next year.

Snider was both embarrassed and incensed by the story, through which ran a fretwork of innuendo, implication, and threat: Snider could not hit left-handers; in the heat of a pennant race, Snider was not expending his greatest efforts; after three productive seasons he was still considered a "potential star" by the Dodgers; he was facing a salary cut next year; the team was considering the possibility of trading him.

The subject of this inflammatory tale sought out the writer and demanded to know the source. Gaven wouldn't tell. Snider then went to the most likely source, Dressen. But the skipper had so much on his mind that he couldn't remember what, if anything, he had said to Gaven a few days before. The clever Charlie pointed out that there were no direct

quotes in the story, making the subtle suggestion that maybe the whole thing had been breathed to life in Gaven's imagination, which Snider knew was not likely.

The real explanation for the story reflected the style of the times and existing journalistic mores. It was not uncommon in those days of dictatorial ownership for the club to communicate with a player through the newspapers (a later-day exponent of this is the Yankees George Steinbrenner), nor was it unknown for a writer to oblige the team and allow himself to be the conduit (though in this particular instance there is no clear indication that this is what happened). In those years, with the club exercising complete leverage, threats of salary cuts and trades were not taken lightly by players. It is unlikely that this kind of tactic would have worked with a Robinson, say, or a Hodges, but the Duke was a different type. The front office apparently felt he still had insecurities they could tap.

A gleeful Snider can't restrain himself as Joe Black retires the last Yankees batter in Brooklyn's 1952 World Series opening-game victory at Ebbets Field.

If the story was indeed a plant, then it was a successful one, for when Snider returned to the lineup he began hitting and didn't stop for the rest of the season. The Duke, always a good money player, was so torrid down the stretch in leading the team to the pennant that Walter O'Malley, always the wiliest of men, reportedly said to Gaven after the clinching that the story had "won the pennant for us."

The Dodgers lost the Series to the Yankees in six, but this time Snider's World Series dream was handsomely embroidered. His home run drove in the winning runs in Game 1, and in Game 4 his hits drove in the tying run in the seventh inning and the winning run

*The Duke just popped
one.*

in the eleventh. Overall, he batted .345 and tied Babe Ruth and Lou Gehrig with four home runs in a World Series.

In 1953, Snider doubled his home run output, soaring from 21 to 42, drove in 126 runs, and batted .336. The rest was repetition—another pennant, another six-game defeat to the Yankees, and another good Series for Snider, who batted .320.

In 1954, with Mays back and exploding to sudden stardom, Snider had his greatest sea-

son, hitting 40 home runs, driving in 130 runs, and batting .341—losing the batting title on the last day of the season to Mays.

And still there were those who maintained that Snider could and should be better, and those who said he would, if only he tried harder. Before the opening of the 1955 season, *Look* magazine ran an article on Snider by sportswriter Tim Cohane entitled "He Reaches for Greatness." The article ranged through the entire Snider spectrum, lauding his abilities,

Five who swelled the cheers of Brooklyn in the 1950s (left to right): *Snider, Hodges, Robinson, Reese, and Campanella.*

referring to his early tendencies to swing at bad balls, his difficulties with left-handed pitching, touched certain career highs and lows, and ended with this sentence: "If they should some day hang Snider's plaque in Cooperstown, the presentation speech will be an empty one if it doesn't include this sentiment: 'The Duke got here the hard way.'" (Also included in the article was this: "Yet, it's a fact—which irritated him for a time—that his biggest headline splashes had to await the heralded return of Mays from service to the New York Giants and the subsequent daily features comparing him with Willie.")

Snider was twenty-eight years old now and had been Brooklyn's regular center fielder for

six years. After his 1953 and 1954 seasons, to say that he was "reaching for greatness" was at that moment placing an intolerable burden upon him. But this had been Snider's burden from the beginning. The expectations, high to begin with, were constantly being dialed higher. The better he got, the greater the expectations grew, and now they included the need to exceed or at least match the standards that Mays was setting, and these, according to the New York writers, had no visible limit.

He was, Snider said, being "squeezed from the outside and pressing on the inside." The fans, he said, knew only what they read, and the natural predisposition was to believe it.

A couple of ace lefties: Veteran Preacher Roe (left) *and young Johnny Podres.*

Snider at home plate in Ebbets Field was the embodiment of power, and the fans came to watch it explode; and when it didn't, the disappointment, because of those high expectations, was keen, and sometimes loud.

One night at Ebbets Field, while trying to break loose from a nagging slump, Snider heard a lot of booing. It was unusual for the home fans to direct disparaging noises at one of their own. Robinson was sometimes booed at home, but that was because he was Robinson and all that went with it. Long-memoried Dodgers fans cannot recall Campanella being booed, nor Furillo, and surely not Reese, nor Hodges either, despite some horrendous

slumps. But that night the Duke heard it, and worse, listened to it. Felt it.

Seething in the clubhouse after the game, Snider suddenly erupted in a brief, pointed diatribe. These were the worst fans in baseball, said the Duke, to the amusement of his teammates and the cocked ears of the writers.

"You want us to print that?" one of the writers asked, as if trying to throw a warning. (It was a different journalism in those days, the press often playing ego to a player's id.)

"Damn right," Snider said. "They're the lousiest fans in baseball, and I want you to say that I said so."

So authorized, the writers duly reported the

The Yankees (left) *and the Dodgers lining up at Ebbets Field before the start of the third game of the 1953 World Series. It was in this game that Carl Erskine (foreground)* beat the Yankees 3–2 and established a Series record with 14 strikeouts.

Duke's fulminations in the next day's papers. If Snider expected a chastened ballpark the following night, he was wrong. The announcement of his name and his appearance at home plate signaled cascades of disapproving noises. He may have been family, but these fans took pride in their fealty, and they let their cherished center fielder know he was out of order. There was only one way to silence the catcalls, and that night Snider was up to it. He hoisted a couple of window breakers over the right-field fence, smashed a line drive or two, and by evening's end all was forgiven. A slight misunderstanding in the

family had been smoothed over. Dodgers fans had too much affection in their hearts for their boys. Nevertheless, the Duke, the most gifted of that superb team of future Hall of Famers, remained the wayward one.

As far as many Dodgers fans were concerned, there was something undefinably elusive about their center fielder. It wasn't anything meaningful or significant; it didn't detract a bit from what he did on the field. It was just enough to leave him in their minds in an incomplete state. They felt they knew Reese, Campanella, Robinson, Erskine, Newcombe, even the businesslike Furillo and the taciturn Hodges. But the Duke, no, not entirely. With all of that talent and with those wholesome good looks, he should have been perfect in every respect, he should have radiated messages back up to the fans, as his predecessor Reiser had. You saw Pistol Pete out there in 1941 and 1942, in the fullness of his brief prime, and you felt you knew this boy, knew just what he was feeling and thinking out there on the green grass. But the Duke? No, not quite.

Something about that marvelous athlete gnawed at you. There was that talk about his aversion to facing left-handers. (Pistol Pete, in an interview given a few years before his death in 1981, said that he—a left-handed batter—wished he could have batted against Koufax when both were in their prime, "just

Snider coming in after hitting one of his 11 World Series homers. This one took place at Ebbets Field in Game 4 of the 1953 Series. Carl Furillo (6) and the batboy congratulate him; Yankees catcher Yogi Berra watches umpire Art Gore put a new ball in play.

Second baseman Jim (Junior) Gilliam.

to see what it was like.") A magazine story had Snider attributing his temperament to the fact of having been an only child and being spoiled by his parents, a statement he later angrily and vehemently denied ever having made. And there were those ongoing rainy-day stories about untapped talent and un-realized potential, which left their implications trailing behind.

Those Dodgers were part of the Borough of Brooklyn in more ways than one. In those days of greater intimacy, without the social stratification imposed by the extravagant salaries of later years, the players were neighbors of the fans, they lived in the same buildings, on the same streets. They rode the subways or carpooled through Brooklyn byways to Ebbets Field. They were visible playing with their children in the Parade Grounds or Prospect Park or pushing shopping carts along the aisles of the A&P. Snider, Rube

Gil Hodges (left) and Carl Furillo embracing Johnny Podres after the young lefty pitched Brooklyn to its only World Series victory over the Yankees in 1955.

Dodgers manager Walter Alston, who replaced Dressen in 1954.

Walker, Carl Erskine, and Pee Wee Reese and their families lived in Bay Ridge. Gil Hodges lived on Bedford Avenue, Jackie Robinson in East Flatbush. Johnny Podres lived in the Hotel Bossert, Joe Black in the St. George. When the 1979 Pittsburgh Pirates proclaimed themselves "family," the reference was to a close-knit team; in Brooklyn in the 1950s, the reference was more expansive, embracing players, team, fans, an entire geographic area.

In May 1956, Snider committed a form of heresy. The title of the article that appeared that month in *Collier's* magazine told it all: "I Play Baseball for Money—Not Fun." ("By Duke Snider with Roger Kahn." Kahn was later to commemorate that entire Dodgers team in his brilliant *The Boys of Summer*.)

Yankees fans, rooting for something that seemed more corporate machine than baseball team anyway, barely took notice of the piece. Giants fans smirked. In Brooklyn there

was embarrassment. Of course every fan knew that baseball was a business, but it was an intrusive kind of knowledge, an awkward truth that came with the territory, an undermining dollop of reality that impinged upon the game's fantasy world. It was something to know and not be reminded about.

In offering his grainy truths about life in the big leagues, the Duke was actually spreading some needed enlightenment, for the team was now just a little more than a year away from being uprooted and spirited to Los Angeles in the name of greater profits. But that of course was going to be engineered by club owner Walter O'Malley, who was anything but a baseball player (nor even a baseball man in the sense that Rickey and Connie Mack and Clark Griffith were), who was not just a lawyer but one who was a parodist's delight with his round belly, big cigar, and aura of shrewd conviviality. But the Duke? He was doing all those wondrous things just for the money?

Snider reckoned that with salary, World Series share, and endorsements, he had earned in 1955 about fifty thousand dollars, serious money in those days, so much so that the Duke seemed to feel almost apologetic about it, saying, ". . . the pay is good, but they take it out of you in sweat and worry."

"The truth is," Snider wrote, "that life in the major leagues is far from a picnic. I'm explaining, not complaining, but believe me, even though deep down I know it isn't true, I feel that I'd be just as happy if I never played another baseball game again."

Snider presented a litany of reasons for his feelings. There was the travel, those interminable train rides during which sleep and proper rest were difficult to come by. There was the mixed schedule of day and night games, which made sensible, balanced eating a problem. There was the "sniping"—from the manager, from fans, from the press. And there was the resentment for being a target for missiles hurled from the stands—he enumerated skate keys, marbles, and beer cans.

Jackie Robinson stealing home. Furillo jumps out of the way.

Once upon a time, when he was a boy in California, Snider said, he dreamed about playing in a World Series. "Last autumn, when I played in my fourth World Series, I was still dreaming. Only the dream had changed. While we were beating the Yankees, I was dreaming about being a farmer." He was looking ahead, he said, to the end of his career and settling down to raising avocados in California.

Snider's dose of reality intruded upon what was supposed to be a special, unspoiled world in the heart of American society. He had dared walk through the temple with muddy shoes, and in those years the temple was still being defended by sportswriters accustomed to shielding the game and the image it sought to project of itself. Because the voice in the article belonged to Snider, it provided further evidence for many writers that here was a spoiled, unappreciative young man who already had a reputation for sulking and complaining.

Generally overlooked or ignored in the noisy response from the defenders of the faith was the candor with which Snider was speaking. He was telling anyone who cared to listen that big-league baseball was not the pure and joyous swath through life it had always been

Some real heavy timber gathering around National League President Warren Giles at the 1956 All-Star Game in Washington, D.C. (left to right): Willie Mays, Ted Kluszewski, Giles, Duke Snider, Stan Musial.

presented as being. There was another side to one of America's most glamorous and envied professions—the tedium of constant stop-and-go travel, the family separations it entailed, the vexing irregularities in life-style it imposed, the callousness of fans, the unyielding pressure to produce, and the bitter frustrations and consequences of failure. Like it or not, Snider was saying, baseball existed in the real world, like everything else. And there was hardly a ballplayer who would have disagreed.

There was also a certain poignance adrift in the article that few chose to take note of.

Snider had dreamed the dream of American youth and pursued it and finally realized it with a fullness given to few, only to find that even fulfilled dreams came with raw edges. Success did not insure one against worry and pain and injury and loneliness; if anything, success in America's game only made those things a greater and more constant part of one's workaday world, and speaking candidly about them was taken as a lack of grace.

Among Dodgers fans the article caused more dismay than indignation. They would, of course, stand behind their center fielder, and now more so than ever, with Mays having hit

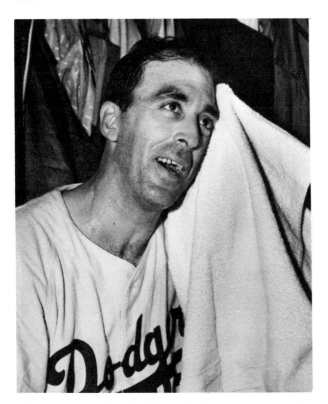

Former New York Giant, Dodgers nemesis Sal Maglie, who joined the Brooks in 1956 and helped pitch them to a pennant.

51 home runs the year before and Mantle beginning to smash his way to what would be a Triple Crown season.

The day the *Collier's* article appeared on the newsstands, four young Brooklyn fans gathered in the local candy store to read it. When the reading had been completed, each spoke a sentence:

"He never said it."

"He did it for the money."

"He doesn't mean it."

"What's avocados?"

Snider remained singular and uncompromising throughout the stardust years in Brooklyn, never quite able, it seemed, to shed completely a gloss of immaturity. Being unable, or unwilling, to conceal his feelings made him vulnerable to his teammates' raillery. A sulking Snider in the clubhouse was a choice target for the rough, chiding humor that passes between athletes.

"Who stole his lollipop?"

"Hey, who's got the Duke's lolly?"

Not even a victory, some teammates said, could assuage a Snider who had taken a collar.

"He was a perfectionist," Hodges said. "We all tried our best, of course, but we were realistic about things. Good days and bad days—you had to balance them out. I don't think Duke was able to do that. When he was going well, he was excited about it, more excited probably than any player I've ever seen. Then, when things turned the other way for a while, as they will, he didn't seem to know how to handle it. As good as he was—and he was great—it bothered him that he couldn't show it every day."

Another source of irritation for Snider was the accusation that he couldn't hit left-handed pitching. When a lefty was starting against them—and with that right-handed-hitting lineup it was not often—teammates recalled a grousing Duke yelling at them to "get that guy out of there." And usually they did. That lineup consumed left-handers like so many hors d'oeuvres, until even the masterful Warren Spahn was seldom risked against them.

The Duke worried too much about his home runs and his batting average, some of the Dodgers said. Well, surely they all worried about their production, as well they might, for there were no multi-year guaranteed contracts back then, and there was a vast farm system coughing up a steady stream of talented and ambitious young ballplayers. The Duke's problem was that he worried visibly and out loud. Also, he believed there was more pressure on him because of those tremendous expectations he had always aroused. Unlike Campanella or Hodges or the others, it seemed he was not allowed a slump. That brigade of writers, who had stung him in the past, was ready to sting again; always ready, he said, to stretch "the truth to back up what they call an 'angle.'" And too often the angle was that Duke Snider was not realizing his potential, as though potential were a tangible thing they could see waiting somewhere untouched and unclaimed.

It's the last day of the 1956 season and the Dodgers need the game to clinch the pennant. Snider just hit a three-run homer in the bottom of the first, and his teammates can't wait for him to reach the dugout. Duke added another homer later in the game as the Dodgers won their final Brooklyn pennant.

In 1955, Snider put together yet another sparkling season. He batted .309, hit 42 home runs, and drove in a career-high, league-leading 136 runs. And as the Dodgers went on to defeat the Yankees in seven games for their first (and only) Brooklyn World Championship, the big siege gun was Duke Snider. For the second time he hit four home runs in World Series competition, tying the record he already held jointly with Ruth and Gehrig. His long-balling in Games 4 and 5 provided his team with its victory margins, setting the stage for Brooklyn's long-sought championship.

In 1956 it was another September without slack or respite for Dodgers fans as their team ran another one of those taut races they had

become so familiar with. For the fifth time in eleven years the Dodgers made the final game the game of decision. In circumstances similar to those of 1949, they held a one-game advantage over their pursuers, this time the Milwaukee Braves. The Dodgers were playing at home against the Pittsburgh Pirates.

In 1949, Snider had driven across the winning run in the tenth inning; in 1950 he had almost singled in the run that would have given the club a tie for the pennant; in 1952 and again in the 1955 World Series he had delivered booming hits in the clutch, deliveries made in the heat of drenching pressure. And in 1956, once again at the foot of the rainbow, Duke Snider rose to the occasion. In

Duke Snider in 1957, the final Brooklyn year.

the bottom of the first inning he sent a packed Ebbets Field into fevers of excitement with a resounding three-run homer, his 42d of the season. Later in the game, he launched his 43d—a league-leading total. In the seventh inning he made a leaping catch of a drive to the center-field wall to put the quietus to a Pirates rally. Guided by Snider's heroics, the Dodgers won the game 8–6 and with it their ninth and final pennant.

After four straight plus-.300 seasons, Snider fell to .292 that year, but he had 101 runs batted in and those 43 league-leading home runs, and in addition led the league in slugging percentage. His all-around statistics were superior to Mays's, but it was in 1956 that the third entry in New York's center field sweepstakes made his presence felt with sizzling impact. This was Mantle's Triple Crown season, and he took his titles decisively: .353 batting average, 52 home runs, 130 runs batted in. In the Dodgers-Yankees World Series

matchup, which the Yankees took in seven, Mantle hit three home runs to Snider's one.

In 1955, Mantle had served notice by leading the American League with 37 home runs; but that was the year Mays hit 51 and drove in 127 runs and Snider hit 42 and drove in 136. In 1956, however, the Yankees Triple Crown was an achievement that had eluded even Ruth and DiMaggio (Gehrig had done it once). Nor did anyone consider it a fluke season (the sort of disdainful skepticism Maris would endure five years later). As a matter of fact, this very thing had been forecast for Mantle from the time he appeared in his first spring camp in 1951. For Mickey, it was a season that crested year after year of steady improvement. His titanic home runs had been measured, his speed down the first-base line clocked. It was almost as though destiny had been taking his measurements for size.

In 1957 Snider tied Ralph Kiner's National League record by hitting 40 or more home runs for a fifth year in a row. Otherwise it was a fall-off year for the Duke and one of dismal uncertainties for the Dodgers. Snider dipped to a .274 batting average and 92 runs batted in, only the second time in eight years he failed to clear the 100 mark in RBIs. In the Polo Grounds, Mays batted .333, hit 35 home runs, and drove in 97 runs. In Yankee Stadium, Mantle followed his big year with a .365 batting average, 34 home runs, and 94 runs batted in—those latter two figures deflated considerably by 146 bases on balls. (Opposing pitchers just didn't want to pitch to Mickey anymore. In contrast, Snider drew over 100 walks in a season just once, as did Mays. Mantle was to draw over 100 walks in a season ten times.)

It was the last time the three great center fielders ran in head-to-head competition. Snider and the Dodgers would open the 1958 season in Los Angeles, Mays and the Giants in San Francisco, five hundred miles apart but linked always now by a few years of tandem stardom and by the sweet incursions of memory.

The departure of the Dodgers from Brooklyn was a wrenching experience for a city, a borough, for neighborhoods, streets, and playgrounds. "We lost them all at once," a Dodgers fan lamented. Something that had always been there, something that had always added character to the return of spring and depth to the long warm days of summer, was now gone. "We even missed the Giants," another Dodgers fan admitted, not unreasonably. "I mean, what the hell, they'd always been part of it, too." Part of it—part of something that had become tribal, ritualistic, part of something that had been long accepted and cherished, upon which one had become accustomed to spending time, energy, and the full spectrum of emotion.

Part of an honored New Year's Day tradition for several young Brooklyn fans (they lived in Queens, actually) was to pile in a car and drive past Ebbets Field. Undeterred by the move to Los Angeles, in fact still in a state of disbelief, they upheld the tradition one last time on January 1, 1958.

Driving down Bedford Avenue, they saw the light towers first, poised against the gray January sky, then the right-field wall with its screen topping. They stared at the old abandoned structure from Sullivan Place and then from Cedar Place, which paralleled the left-field line. It was all still in place inside, the empty dugouts, the ice-cold seats, the dead grass, a chill wind circling through it all like a ghostly ambience. It used to look asleep in the winter, like some hibernating thing. But now it looked dead, caught in a warp between time spent and time unspent, memories born and memories adrift; a mastodon frozen in Siberian ice. On other New Year's Day pilgrimages they could imagine life behind the walls, lights going up on a warm summer's night, the unique sound of a struck baseball, and the huge impersonal roar from the grandstands. The promise had always been there. But not anymore.

There would be no more Brooklyn Dodgers. They were fixed in completion now, a finished portrait. The best could no longer be bettered. And the best of all Brooklyn center fielders would always be that graceful dynamo who had roamed the bright green grass of Ebbets Field from 1949 to 1957, coincident with the greatest of Dodgers teams. A Duke. Maybe not one listed in *Burke's Peerage*, but within the constituency of baseball, genuine royalty.

CHAPTER THREE

Becoming a major star in Brooklyn Dodgers history meant establishing your own high standard and maintaining it. Compared to that of many other teams, the historical competition was thin. The major Dodgers stars (other than pitchers) had been Zack Wheat, a superb .300 hitter of the Wilbert Robinson era, but not a long-baller; Babe Herman, a lusty hitter but notoriously unpredictable in the field; Dixie Walker, a sharp-hitting outfielder, but actually better known for his popularity than for any particular achievements; and Pete Reiser, his career aborted by injuries after a few mercurial seasons. It was Duke Snider who finally set the standard at all points of the compass for Brooklyn Dodgers stars.

Becoming a major star in New York Yankees history, however, meant climbing a much more demanding and steeper path. It meant meeting the standards of Ruth, Gehrig, and DiMaggio, and not just statistically either, for this trio of precursors had by one means or another surpassed the eminence of statistics and become part of the national consciousness.

With its reputation of urban swagger, and because of decades of Yankees dominance, New York was both threat and oppressor to baseball fans around the country. Consequently, a Yankees superstar carried weights and obligations unlike those of any other major-league ballplayer. Fascination with the Yankees star of the day was always keen—the menacing is always more interesting than the benevolent—and the more brute power the star demonstrated, the greater the menace, the more involving the fascination. For thirty years those stars had been named Ruth, Gehrig, and DiMaggio, thunderbolts who had passed into American folklore. New York as a city and the Yankees as a baseball team might have been abhorred for their arrogance and their success, but fans never ceased coming out in record numbers to see that team play, for they always knew that there would be one among the nine who embodied the power and the might, who was New York in one of its most compelling representations. Such a player had to be stunningly unique, able to penetrate the mesh of resentment and through

51

Phoenix, 1951.

Mickey Charles Mantle, shortstop for the Joplin club of the Western Association, 1950.

breathtaking heroics disarm it. Like Ruth, Gehrig, and DiMaggio, he had to be able to evoke the aura of baseball's soul, the secret of its enchantment, the nobility of its drama. In time, a fourth Yankee, Mickey Mantle, was to achieve this rarefied stature.

He was born in Oklahoma, which was distant enough to be considered uncharted territory by many New Yorkers; it was somewhere west of the Hudson River, in another part of the United States, as Arkansas was, and Idaho. The boy had a face and smile that Hollywood once upon a time promoted as typically American, and he even had a catchy name to go with it. There would be no need for sportswriters to coin a "Joltin' Joe" or "Larrupin' Lou," for the boy arrived already alliterative. And that name Mickey was real, too; he had been named after his father's favorite ballplayer, Mickey Cochrane. Mickey Mouse. Mickey Rooney. Mickey Mantle. All quintessentially American, in one way or another. So much of him fit the dream image of what the American hero should be. Handsome, strong, shy, bashful, arriving in New York carrying a cheap suitcase and owner of a single sport jacket, which, one teammate remembered, "looked like it cost seven dollars."

The difference with this particular boy was, instead of getting off a Greyhound and gaping at the tall buildings while his pocket was being picked, he came to town with the New York Yankees, all of nineteen years old and already hailed and trumpeted, beribboned with press clippings heralding him as the next— well, they weren't sure, because according to those early witnesses there had never been anyone like him. He could hit like Ruth, throw like DiMaggio, run like Cobb: as near to an American Superman as you could possibly get. And he was a switch-hitter in the bargain. He sounded like the '27 Yankees reborn into a one-man economy package. And that shy, reticent personality suited the Yankees just fine. They preferred the dignified aloofness of a DiMaggio or a Gehrig to the rollicking tremors of a Ruth.

Old Clark Griffith, owner of the Washington Senators, on the scene for more than a half-century, longer than the American League itself, who had been feeling the Yankees spiked shoe on his neck for decade upon decade, was wryly philosophical about it. The Old Fox knew talent and knew just what he was seeing in the new man. "They lost Ruth and then Gehrig," he said, "and never stopped winning; seemed to get even stronger. Now they're about to lose DiMaggio, and they're not going to miss him either. They've got this new boy."

"The day I was born," Mickey Charles Mantle said, "my father told my mother that he would make me a pro ballplayer." Not just pro but big leaguer, and not just big leaguer but star. You knew that was the dream of Elvin (Mutt) Mantle, ex-semipro pitcher and baseball fan, because fathers don't dream sparingly when it comes to their sons, and because old dead dreams that one once had for oneself don't really die but become resurrected at new opportunities, and especially when one has a son who seems sturdy and inclined; and so into this new container the dream is poured, rejuvenated and as bold as

Mantle in spring training with the Yankees in Phoenix, 1951.

ever. It was Ward Snider and his Duke all over again, but maybe even grittier and more intense this time, because in Commerce, Oklahoma, there seemed only one doomed alternative to not playing in the big leagues.

Mutt's failed dream had sent him through one hardscrabble dead-end job after another and finally four hundred feet underground to the lead and zinc mines that had hollowed out the earth beneath Commerce, where Mickey and his four younger siblings were raised. Mutt worked for the Eagle-Picher Zinc and Lead Company. He was a ground boss, or foreman, having worked his way up from breaking boulders into rocks, minding the mules that hauled laden cars along the underground tracks, hacking at the rich and intractable walls; working in damp, dusty netherworld gloom even as his thoughts soared to the yellow sunshine and green grass of America's game.

The mines were invisible but ubiquitous, part of every personal history in Commerce, a menacing vortex waiting to suck down any man whose fortune it was to be born in the area. (The mines were several hundred feet under the very house in which Mickey lived during his first winters as a Yankee, a threatening pit to snare him if he fell.)

So for Mutt Mantle it was more than simply a baseball fanatic's resolution to see his own furled dream realized in his son; he saw baseball as a means for his son getting the best that life could offer, as perceived from the perspective of a hard-working, still-watered corner of northeast Oklahoma in the times known as the Great Depression. The education was simple and direct, there was but one course of study—baseball—with its various subdivisions: fielding, running, throwing, the subtleties of the game, and most crucially, switch-hitting. A left-handed grandfather threw to the five-year-old right-handed batter, the right-handed father to the little left-handed batter. This was no after-hours frolic either; this was serious business if the boy was to stay out of the mines and know the

Casey Stengel: He had to admit he'd never seen anything like Mickey.

better life. Mutt Mantle's dream may have had its wistful qualities, but it was grounded in a miner's hardheaded realism: *No boy of mine . . .*

Mickey was born on October 20, 1931, in the small town of Spavinaw, Oklahoma, in the northeast corner of the state, almost equidistant from the neighboring states of Missouri, Kansas, and Arkansas. (The family moved to Commerce, forty-five miles to the northeast, when Mickey was still an infant.)

Mutt's dream was abetted by nature, which had conspired with a father's innermost rev-

erie and woven strength and power and speed and matchless coordination into the limbs and fibers of the boy. "Coordination," said Casey Stengel two decades later, watching his prodigy in the batting cage. "You gotta get all them back and shoulder and arm muscles workin' together the second you're puttin' the bat on the ball. That's what he does. That's why the ball disappears so fast."

Even as he hacked at the underground to make it yield its bounty, so did Mutt work diligently and knowingly at shaping and molding his robust firstborn, impelling the

When Mickey joined the team in 1951, he found they already had a couple of boomers: Joe Di-Maggio (left) *and Johnny Mize.*

boy to yield his own ingrained bounties. At six months, the baby was wearing a baseball cap knitted by his mother; at three years he had his own uniform. "I can't remember when I wasn't wearing a glove," he said, "throwing a tennis ball against a wall, or hitting a tennis ball with a bat."

They must have been deeply synergetic exercises, or at least anyway the ones that we know about, the ones involving Ward and Duke Snider and Mutt and Mickey Mantle for instance, because these fathers were stern and demanding taskmasters. It couldn't have been pure baseball for the boys, not all exhilarating and enjoyable rhythms; to the fathers it was an almost mystically calculated design,

of deep commitment, of concentrated building, and if the boy ever demonstrated anything less than total dedication to it, it was not received lightly. When Mutt once caught young Mickey not switch-hitting in a sandlot game, the father ordered the son off the field and sent him home, telling the boy that "unless you switch-hit like I taught you" the boy would never wear a baseball uniform again.

In the classical telling of these stories, the boy rebels against a father's single-minded obsession. But young Duke Snider didn't, nor did young Mickey Mantle. Quite the opposite. They listened and they obeyed and they learned, and they grew to manhood and went on to magnificent careers and then beyond into retirement without the slightest indication of resentment for having had to absorb the full force of a father's dream. Listen to Mantle: "I just wanted to please my father more than anything else." The love and respect he felt for this strong, brawny, remorselessly determined man were, and remain, boundless, which tells us that the boy partook of the father's dream as though it were a shared organism. (Mutt Mantle's death from Hodgkin's disease in 1952, Mickey's second year in the big leagues, only served to sanctify the old dream as the boy went on to embody it with more and more splendor.)

These, of course, are the stories we know about, of talent so great it is able to respond, keep growing and expanding and improving until its capacities and manifestations have filled the furthest contours of the dream and no doubt dazzled even those blood-kindred drill instructors. The other stories, of the sons failing to exceed the modest abilities of their extravagantly dreaming fathers who finally give up in disenchantment, remain blank pages.

An athlete of Mantle's abilities would have made himself prominent in any environment; in Commerce, amid its two thousand people, he was as conspicuous as a sunrise. Along with baseball, he was also a star halfback on the Commerce High team, good enough to have

Mickey at home in Oklahoma after the 1951 season with twin brothers Roy (left) and Ray.

Mantle and his recent bride, Merlyn, packing for spring training in 1952.

drawn scholarship interest from several colleges (he must have been quite a sight, with his speed, breaking loose on an open field). It was while playing football that Mantle suffered the first of the many serious injuries that were to plague his career. One evening during a team scrimmage, he was kicked in the left ankle. What seemed at first a trivial injury quickly worsened. A few nights later a feverish Mantle was rushed to a bone specialist, who lanced the ankle and gave the boy the first of a series of penicillin shots that were to be applied steadily over the next few weeks. Osteomyelitis—a purulent inflammation of the bone—developed, becoming grave enough for the doctor to consider the possibility of amputation. (Mantle records this in his autobiography *The Mick*, written with Herb Gluck.) The condition eventually stabilized itself, however, though it remained always threatening and was considered serious enough for Mickey to be rejected four different times for military service during the Korean War.

Joe DiMaggio.

Yogi Berra.

Mickey was in his third year of high school when his long-ball exploits reached the ears of Yankees scout Tom Greenwade. Greenwade, a shrewd, laconic talent hunter from Willard, Missouri, traveled to Baxter Springs, Kansas, where Mantle was playing in an amateur league game. The scout liked what he saw, but because the boy was still in high school Greenwade was forbidden by baseball law to talk business. But he would be back next year, the scout said, the day Mickey graduated.

Greenwade kept an eye on the calendar, returning immediately upon Mickey's graduation from Commerce High and signing the boy to a contract. Subsequent events have turned the occasion into a historic one, and since it is historic it has been recorded in a number of different versions. One version has Mickey scheduled to play in Baxter Springs, the game being rained out, and Mickey, his father, and Greenwade sitting in the scout's Oldsmobile in the driving rain trying to come to an agreement. In his book, Mickey says the

Gene Woodling.

contract was signed in Coffeyville, Kansas, which is better since it was the birthplace of Walter Johnson. In any event, the constants remain Mutt, Mickey, Greenwade, and the Oldsmobile.

The terms, hammered out by the father and the scout, with the boy sitting silently in the back seat, were, in retrospect, quaintly neat and simple: For signing, Mickey was to receive a bonus of $1,100 and a salary of $140 a month, which was about the going rate in the low minor leagues in those days. The contract called for him to play out the rest of the season (this was in June 1949) with the Independence, Missouri, club in the Class D Kansas-Oklahoma-Missouri League (known in baseball shorthand as the K-O-M League).

He was a shortstop then, and by everyone's testimony, including his own, not a very good one. In 89 games with Independence, he made 47 errors. But he batted .313, hit seven home runs, and drove in 63 runs. A mixed bag of statistics, but statistics are sometimes sec-

ondary in the minor leagues, especially in a boy's first year. Mantle's manager at Independence was former major-league outfielder Harry Craft. Craft's evaluation of the new man gave a pretty clear peek into the future. "Can be a great hitter," Harry wrote to his employers in New York. "Exceptional speed. Attitude excellent. Will go all the way. He has everything to make a great ballplayer."

Tom Greenwade agreed. The tall, sparely built man with the weather-etched face that seems to come with his profession sensed from the beginning what he had lucked into. As early as the spring of 1950, after Mantle had played just a half year of minor-league ball at the lowest classification, Greenwade was positive. There had been a few storybook discoveries by men in his tireless, ever optimistic calling, the kinds of discoveries that validate the dream that every scout packs in his bag each time he leaves home. Yankees scout Paul Krichell seeing Lou Gehrig at Columbia University and Cleveland hunter Cy Slapnicka coming upon Bob Feller among the cornstalks of Iowa were probably the two most legendary sightings. Greenwade was prepared to add a third.

"I know just how Krichell felt the first time he saw Gehrig," Greenwade told a writer in that spring of 1950 (after Mantle had, remember, played just a few months of Class D ball). Krichell had told the story often enough, how the excitement had surged into him and then leveled off into a kind of benign serenity as he sat and watched Gehrig that first time. It seemed to erase from the past all mistakes, disappointments, and injustices. The world held bounties indeed if only you were in the right place at the right time, in this case on the campus of a great university, four miles from the Yankees home office.

"Krichell said," Greenwade went on, "that as a scout he knew he'd never have another moment like it." Nor, probably, would Krichell have hoped for one. It would have been blasphemous. There are certain cups that will stand only one filling.

Hank Bauer.

"I felt the same way when I first saw Mickey Mantle," Greenwade said. "He's going to be one of the all-time greats."

Mickey was promoted just a notch in 1950, assigned to Class C ball with the Joplin, Missouri, club in the Western Association. The eighteen-year-old boy exploded that year, hitting 26 home runs, driving in 136 runs, and batting .383. But more than the statistics, what caught the attention of the big club in New York was the style in which the youngster was accumulating those numbers. The

fans in Joplin and around the league in towns like Muskogee and Topeka and Enid and Salina were getting the feeling that a once-in-a-lifetime phenomenon was orbiting the area according to the dictates of the Western Association schedule, and so they came out and sat in the rickety small-town grandstands and waited for the boy to launch one of his titanic drives or go from first to third before you could blink an eye. And so what if he was still erratic at shortstop, making 55 errors? You could always learn to field; you can't teach a boy to

Mantle has just fallen injured while chasing Mays's fly ball in the second game of the 1951 World Series at Yankee Stadium. That's DiMaggio running up to help.

run like that, or throw like that, or hit a ball so far that years later people would be pointing to the spot.

So that was 1950, the same year that nineteen-year-old Willie Mays broke into pro ball with the New York Giants Trenton, New Jersey, team in the Class B Interstate League, playing in 81 games and batting .353. Twenty-four-year-old Duke Snider had completed his second full year as Brooklyn's regular center fielder, batting .321, third best in the National League.

For decades the Yankees had been taking their spring training in Saint Petersburg, but in 1951 they agreed to a one-year switch of spring camps with the New York Giants. The Giants took over the Saint Petersburg camp, and the Yankees gathered in the Giants facility in Phoenix, Arizona.

Among the nonroster invitees to the Yankees camp was Mantle. The club had already penciled in the youngster for their Binghamton, New York, team in the Class A Eastern League. With a perennially winning team at the top and a widespread farm system crowded with talent, the Yankees had the luxury of being able to bring their young players along with care and diligence. If Mickey did well at Binghamton, the next stop would probably be their Triple-A Kansas City team in the American Association, and then maybe, in 1953, the big team. Water, laconic philosophers are fond of saying, finds its own level. But sometimes there's a riptide in the currents, causing immense disturbances. An inapt metaphor, perhaps, for an occurrence in the Arizona desert; but something of this nature happened in Phoenix in the spring of 1951.

Class C ball or not, Mantle was already regarded as the prize of the farm system, and Stengel and the rest of the Yankees weights-and-measures department wanted a good look before dispatching him to Binghamton. After the first good look, they decided to forget about Binghamton and send him straight to Kansas City, a rather radical decision for the conservative Yankees front office. After a second good look they were enthralled into confusion and frankly didn't know what to do. And they weren't the only ones who were watching this boy day in and day out with growing wonderment: On hand was the New York press, always a tough-minded, competitive group, always on the lookout for something to capture the interest and stir the imaginations of their baseball-starved readership back home.

They were world champions two years running, those Yankees, and Mickey found himself on the same field with Joe DiMaggio, Yogi Berra, Phil Rizzuto, Allie Reynolds, Vic Raschi, and all the rest. But it was the new boy—so shy, Stengel said, "that he looked at the ground whenever I talked to him, as if afraid his shoes would fall off"—the nineteen-year-old up from Joplin, Missouri, who was going to dominate this camp, as no rookie has dominated a spring camp before or since. What would have been the camp's most steadily flogged theme—would an aching heel cloud what everyone suspected was going to be DiMaggio's retirement year?—soon became of secondary interest. It was sunrise and twilight, both at the same time.

Here was another smart example of Yankees logistics working as it had for thirty years: replacing a Ruth with a DiMaggio, a Dickey with a Berra, a Lazzeri with a Gordon, a Crosetti with a Rizzuto. Each transition smooth

Mantle being carried off the field after his injury in the 1951 Series.

DiMaggio, Mantle, and Williams.

and seamless, hello and good-bye with a single wave of the hand. Rizzuto was an MVP shortstop in 1950, but no matter; the new man was not a big-league shortstop. The gap would be in center field, and the new man had all the tools for that—the speed, the arm, the good baseball instincts.

A Yankees center fielder was expected to hit. DiMaggio's immediate predecessor in the position, Earle Combs, who played from 1924 through 1935, had finished with a .325 lifetime batting average. DiMaggio would finish his own career that year with a .325 lifetime batting average. More than a quarter of a century of sparkling high-caliber consistency from that position. The team was ready to

turn the dial up ahead another fifteen years or so and sit comfortably back.

They watched the new man hit 500-footers right-handed and 500-footers left-handed into the dazzlingly blue southwestern skies. No one had ever seen a single man bring two such loaded cannons to the plate. They watched him race the fastest men in camp and beat them by ten yards, beat them so decisively that the first time it happened the coaches made them line up and do it over again, certain that the others must have stumbled in getting away.

He was a shock to his sixty-one-year-old manager, who thought by now, after following the baseball trails for forty years, from the backwaters to the big leagues, after seeing them all from Cobb and Ruth to DiMaggio and Williams, that he had seen all the magic that could happen on a baseball field. But the old man had to admit that he had never seen anything like this, something so remarkable it seemed almost ingenuous to believe it.

"All I know," Casey Stengel said as Mickey ripped away at a .400 clip in exhibition games, "is that he has me terribly confused and he's getting me more so every day." The boy wasn't ready for the big leagues yet, the skipper said. The boy should have a year of Triple-A ball. "That would be the logical thing," Stengel maintained. "But this kid ain't logical. He's too good. It's very confusing."

He's too good. It was almost as if the old man had discovered a new species, one that contradicted and rebutted everything he had always believed in.

The superlatives being filed from the Yankees camp were whetting the appetites of baseball-starved New Yorkers enduring the irascible snarls of winter's end. All of the writers from all of New York's then many newspapers were unanimous in their gong and cymbal noises. Ruth, Cobb, and DiMaggio all wrapped up in one young man. A Hercules. A Mercury. A Superman. Perfect, just perfect for a city that saw itself as the colossus of cities. Only New York would be able to accommodate so gigantic a talent.

Branch Rickey, running the Pittsburgh Pirates then, took one look at Mantle and handed Yankees co-owner Dan Topping a blank check. "Name your own price," said Mr. Rickey, acknowledged then and always as the indisputable high lama of baseball judgment. Topping laughed and declined. Rickey told a writer, "I've been looking for ballplayers for a long time, and Mantle is the finest prospect I've ever seen. He's my ideal rookie. He's the kind of kid I've always dreamed of finding. He has that flawless, level swing and the fastest break from the plate I've ever seen."

It was all duly reported back to New York. The stories were read in living rooms, barber

Left-hander Whitey Ford, greatest of all Yankees pitchers. Along with Billy Martin he was Mantle's closest friend on the Yankees.

shops, saloons, on subways and buses. When the writers tired of describing home runs that cut jet stream arcs through the skies, they turned to the boy himself. He was as perfect off the field as on: "shy," "modest," with the physique of "an Adonis," with "corn-colored" hair, blue eyes, and a smile "capable of lighting up a room."

The Yankees agonized. New York or Kansas City? Stengel continued to maintain that Mickey "should have a year of Triple-A under his belt." But, "You writers have blowed him up so much that I have to take him to New York. I'm not blaming you—he's everything you say he is—but it doesn't figure that he's ready. Then again, nothing he does figures."

But for Stengel, a canny old baseball junkie with a keen sense of the parallels and continuities of his game, the fact of Mickey Mantle was marked with a special opportunity. Stengel's managerial idol had always

Martin (left) *and Mantle.*

been John McGraw, for whom Casey had played in the early 1920s. It was part of baseball lore how in 1925 the sixteen-year-old Mel Ott traveled up from Gretna, Louisiana, to New York City to see John McGraw at the Polo Grounds and ask for a tryout. In acquiescing, McGraw was doing a favor for an old friend who had recommended the boy as a prospect. McGraw quickly sized up the kid who strode into a pitch with his right leg cocked in the air and who had a beautifully level and powerful swing, and realized that this was what managers wait for—that totally unknown, perfectly exquisite young talent, a jewel found among the sands. Sixteen years

old or not, McGraw would not allow the boy to be sent to the minor leagues, where someone might tamper with that highly singular and unorthodox batting style. (Ott remained with the Giants, as player and manager, until 1948, retiring with 511 home runs, at the time the most in National League history.)

"He told me once," Stengel said, speaking of McGraw, "that you can spend your whole life in this game and not have that sort of thing happen to you. But he said it *could* happen and that you had to keep your eyes open all the time."

Mickey Mantle was going to be Casey's Mel Ott, and then some.

Mantle is about to touch home plate after slamming a tremendous grand-slam homer against the Dodgers at Ebbets Field in the fifth game of the 1953 World Series. Waiting to greet Mickey are Joe Collins (15), Hank Bauer (9), and Yogi Berra (8). The catcher is Roy Campanella, the umpire Bill Grieve.

Mantle and Brooklyn's Pee Wee Reese during the 1953 World Series.

So he rode into New York on a tidal wave of publicity to open the 1951 season, heralded as the eventual replacement for the man who had been the most flawless of all ballplayers. Even before having played a single major-league game, Mantle was being taken at face value; he was being asked to endorse baseball gloves, cigarettes, bubble gum. He felt "surrounded," he said, and no doubt was, for that was what happened to celebrities in New York. Still, this was a pragmatic boy, more concerned with the practical than with the trappings of coronation. "What I was worrying about," he said, "was going back on a line drive and how to cut down on my strikeouts." He did not know, of course, and surely had no way of knowing, that he was walking on a landscape of trap doors; that included in this city's boundless generosity, abundant offerings, and shrewd affection were veins of cold cynicism, skepticism, disapproval, and rejection that ran deeper and darker than the lead and zinc mines of Commerce.

Probably more than anything else, Mickey felt the pressure that was coming, unwittingly of course, from center field. The DiMaggio aura was not lost on Mantle. Standing in right field on opening day at Yankee Stadium, in front of more people than had seen him play the year before in all the Joplin home games put together, the rookie had two nagging concerns—that in hawking a fly ball he might run into Joe and knock him down, or that he might make an embarrassing error in front of the great man.

Nor had Joe made it easy for the boy. The DiMaggio reputation was vast, and somewhere inside it lay the enigmatic, self-protective man himself. Eyeing his teammate-legend in spring training, the boy from Commerce remembered "that he looked like a senator," and that "he looked like you needed an invitation to approach him." The shy Mantle never asked DiMaggio for advice; the aloof DiMaggio never offered it. It was simply a matter of two enclosed personalities, and this was too bad, for in the unanimous opinion of DiMaggio's teammates, Joe was always willing to "cross the street to help you," if only you asked.

Mickey opened the season hitting well, and this along with all of the previous publicity (and the public's curiosity about him), got him invitations to such television staples of the day as "The Ed Sullivan Show," "Break the Bank," and "We the People." He was "The Sweet Switcher" in the long articles the New York press kept churning out about him. The more they wrote, the more the gap between fact and fiction began to widen. They reported that he made a lot of money, that he frequented nightclubs, that he spent extravagantly on clothes. The tone of the stories sometimes made him sound like a young man diving foolishly into the New York fleshpots. The fact was, none of the stories were true. For those first few months Mickey was living alone in a small room in the Concourse Plaza Hotel in the Bronx, taking his meals in inelegant cafeterias, lying abed and listening to the elevated trains roar and clatter through the night, like a fugitive in a gritty 1940s suspense movie. But too many writers, in on the creation of Mantle that spring, were now trying to wedge him into a certain image, as though it were incumbent upon them to keep re-creating and redefining him. Again the boy was feeling the weight of the New York syndrome; it wasn't enough merely to be a star or an impending star, one had to be one with flair and style, and if you lacked the extra dimensions or the grand gestures, they would be imposed on you.

After his promising start, Mickey went into a slump. The trouble was mostly from the left side, where they were eating him up with high inside fastballs.

Raucous noises began coming out of the right-field stands, where the loudmouths seemed to have seated themselves simply for the joy of thundering at Mickey. "Go back to Oklahoma!" was one of the kinder things he heard (although for certain red-blooded New Yorkers, this was probably a very serious imprecation). He worried about striking out so often, worried about his fielding, worried about what his teammates were thinking. The writers' reluctance to let go of him made it worse. He continued to fascinate them. No matter who the hero of the game might be, they came at Mickey for postgame interviews, even if only to ask, "What kind of pitch did you strike out on?"

As the slump continued, his confidence waned. For the first time in his life he was unable to take full command on an athletic field. He was undergoing in the spring and early summer of 1951 what Duke Snider had endured a few years earlier in Brooklyn. But for Mickey it was worse. Though heralded, Snider had not come up in the same glare of publicity as Mickey. No rookie had. The difference between the warrants of the young

Gil McDougald, who joined the Yankees with Mantle in 1951 and gave the club a decade of solid play at second, short, and third.

Snider and the young Mantle was simple but telling: Snider will be. Mantle is.

Another difference was that Mantle was playing for the Yankees, the most famous and representative of the New York teams, and therefore bigger, louder, more conspicuous, more feared, more disliked, more everything. Also, the Yankees were striving for a third consecutive pennant; they could not afford to be patient with a struggling young player (always a club characteristic, in fact, then and now). Nor, with outfielders DiMaggio, Gene

Woodling, Hank Bauer, and Jackie Jensen, did they *need* Mantle.

It meant a king-sized admission from Stengel and the team hierarchy that they had been wrong in rushing the youngster, but in mid-July an unhappy and embarrassed Stengel informed Mickey of the demotion to Kansas City. The Yankees, who had reduced Mantle's status to that of part-time player, wanted him to play every day, which was no longer feasible in New York. Mickey's .264 batting average and the fact that he trailed only Berra

Yankees shortstop Phil Rizzuto.

for the team lead in runs batted in would have kept him in the lineup of most other clubs, but not the Yankees, whose standards were demanding and tolerance low.

Confused and dejected, Mickey went to Kansas City (where his manager, George Selkirk, could have told him something about New York pressure: A highly capable Yankees right fielder of the 1930s, Selkirk was the man who had replaced Babe Ruth in the position, even wearing Ruth's No. 3).

Mantle's slump continued through his opening games in Kansas City. So did his confusion and dejection, which quickly festered into despair and total loss of confidence. It provoked a call to his father at the Eagle-Picher mines. He was ready to give up and come home, Mickey told his father.

Five hours later, an aroused Mutt Mantle appeared at Mickey's hotel in Kansas City. Without ceremony, the lead and zinc miner from Commerce wanted to know: Had he raised a man or a coward? Mutt tore into his son as only a proud, loving, and bitterly disappointed father could. At the end of the tirade Mutt said that if Mickey wanted to give up, then fine, he would help the boy pack. And then the threat that was the tough-minded miner's long nightmare: Mickey could go to work in the mines with him.

Mutt's arraignment of his son was effective. Both probably knew it would be. Mickey went to work all right, not in the mines at Commerce, but at home plate for Kansas City. In 40 games he drove in 50 runs, hit 11 home runs, and batted .361. By the end of August he was back in New York, properly chastened and ready.

In October he was playing in his first World Series, standing in right field when the Series opened against the Giants in Yankee Stadium, having completed his interrupted major-league season with a .267 batting average and 13 home runs. Both figures were slightly better than DiMaggio's for the same categories, and if Joe hadn't already made up his mind to retire, then the first subpar year of

his career would surely have pushed him in that direction.

Thus Mickey's season was ending as it had begun, standing in right field in Yankee Stadium, to the left of the great DiMaggio, who was, even after months as teammates, still something of an enigma to the rookie, and of course still something of an icon, too, not only magisterial as a ballplayer but also as a personality. So, when in the fifth inning of the second game of the 1951 World Series a fly ball was hoisted into right center and both DiMaggio and Mantle were going for it, Mickey slammed on the brakes the moment he heard Joe calling for it, remembering the earlier injunction: *You don't run into Joe DiMaggio.* The instant he stopped, Mantle felt a searing pain in his right knee. His spikes had caught on the cover of a drain hole in the outfield grass. He went down with startling suddenness and lay there in such absolute stillness that for a moment some of the spectators thought he had been shot.

Mickey watched the rest of the Series on television from a room in Lenox Hill Hospital, resting an injured knee that had been operated on for torn ligaments.

Ironically, the fly ball Mickey was injured chasing had been hit by the other new man in town, the Giants rookie center fielder Willie Mays.

They were the golden rookies of 1951, Mantle and Mays. Willie had joined the Giants in May, coming up from Minneapolis of the American Association (two months before Mickey was optioned down to the same league). Willie had appeared suddenly, and gone on by dint of personality, talent, and a gripping pennant race to establish vivid credentials for himself. Willie was credited by many people with having been the catalyst in the Giants astonishing pennant victory. There was no question that without him the Giants would not have won it; in Yankee Stadium there was little doubt that with or without Mantle, the Yankees would still have won it.

In 1952 DiMaggio was gone, but Mickey

Mantle.

was not yet the center fielder; Jackie Jensen was. Early in May, however, the Yankees made a significant commitment to the boy from Oklahoma; they traded the highly regarded Jensen to Washington, and soon after, Mantle became the Yankees center fielder.

It was still too early for anyone to start thinking of New York's three center fielders in any comparative or competitive way. For one thing, Mays entered the army in May 1952, not to return until 1954; for another, Snider was a fully established star now. And while Mantle was considered by most baseball people to have almost limitless potential, to large segments of Yankees fans (many of whom resented the suggestion that the revered DiMaggio could be replaced) he remained a dubious character, a broken promise.

What was significant about Mantle in those prelude years, however, was the attention he drew. Though still far from major stardom, the quiet youngster nevertheless continued

to be an intriguing, widely publicized athlete. Unfortunately, much of the attention he drew was on the negative side, centering on his draft status.

Mickey had been classified 4-F by the Selective Service Board of Ottawa County in Oklahoma. That was in December 1950. When he became a Yankee in the spring of 1951, the war in Korea was in full blazing fury, and young men everywhere were being drafted. The sight of this impressive physical specimen in the Yankees outfield (along with all of that relentless publicity) spurred angry letters to newspapers, to Mickey's local draft board, to Selective Service Headquarters in Washington, to members of the president's cabinet, to the president himself. Recalled and reexamined in Tulsa in April, Mantle was again deferred because of the chronic osteomyelitis in his ankle. ("He has to shoot the Commies, not kick them to death," went one disgruntled refrain.) Twice being turned down by Selective Service still did not placate the superpatriots. The resentment continued, there were more letters, including some of an odious nature to Mantle himself, and two more examinations were made, in August 1951 and November 1952, each with the same result. Blameless in the matter, Mantle was ready to serve, but the military wanted no part of him.

So even though the draft boards were making sound, objective decisions about him, Mantle still had to listen to shouted accusations of "coward," "Commie," and other crackbrained epithets. "He never complained about the unfairness of it all," a teammate recalled. "He heard them all right, and it had to hurt. But he never complained." It was to become one of the hallmarks of his later superstardom—never complaining, in spite of injuries and pain and steady doses of hard luck.

In 1952, Mantle's first full season, the Yankees took their fourth consecutive pennant and World Series, tying the achievement of Joe McCarthy's 1936–39 teams. Mickey's year was solid, if unspectacular: a .311 batting average, 23 home runs, 87 runs batted in, marred by a league-leading 111 strikeouts. His figures were comparable to Snider's that year, but Duke outgunned him in the Series, hitting a record-tying four home runs to Mickey's two.

Despite Mantle's fine season, he still was not the preeminent Yankee—Yogi Berra led the club in home runs and runs batted in, and with as many at bats struck out just 24 times.

A year later, when Stengel had finally out-McGrawed and out-McCarthyed those illus-trious precedent setters with a fifth consecutive pennant and World Championship, Mantle, despite another productive outing (.295 batting average, 21 home runs, 92 runs batted in), was still topped by Berra in home runs and RBIs, while Yogi and two other Yankees batted higher than Mickey. As far as Snider was concerned, not even the most passionate Mantle devotee would have dared a comparison; Duke batted .336, hit 42 home runs, and drove in 126 runs.

Nevertheless, it was in 1953, early in the season, that Mantle achieved one of those

Mantle in spring training at the Yankees Saint Petersburg camp in the early 1950s.

sudden, awesome eruptions that were the mark of the legend-to-be, and one of the center-pieces of the legend itself.

The date was April 17. The Yankees were playing the Washington Senators in Griffith Stadium. Mantle came to bat in the fifth inning against southpaw Chuck Stobbs. Stobbs got a strike across on Mickey and then aimed a fastball designed as strike two. Mickey swung and connected, mightily, bashing one of baseball's landmark home runs. Unlike Bobby Thomson's, it did not win a pennant; unlike Bill Mazeroski's, it did not win a World Series. If it has kinship in baseball history, it is with Ruth's "called shot" in the 1932 World Series; but where Ruth's clout crowned a legend, Mantle's was the launching of one. Of all the fabled home runs in baseball history, Mantle's alone stands for something other than dramatic victory. This particular cannon shot stands for might and power; it is its own colossal symbol.

From home plate to the foot of the left-field bleachers was a distance of 391 feet. It was another 69 feet to the rear of the bleachers, where the ball went over at a height estimated at more than 55 feet. From the rear of the bleachers to where the ball landed in the

The most powerful rip in baseball.

A view of Griffith Stadium and the left-field bleachers over which Mantle's 565-foot home run rocketed.

backyard of a house was paced off at another 105 feet, making it a grand total of 565 feet from point of impact.

It was an extraordinary blow, for anyone; but coming from the bat of the youngster for whom this sort of artillery work had been lavishly predicted, it was portentous, like the first shell fired over a frontier. It was recognized as something more than a once-in-a-lifetime blast, too; *The Sporting News* gave the story full-page coverage in its April 29 issue, beginning with three tiers of headlines:

MANTLE MAKES HOME RUN HISTORY AT 21
Power Kings of the Past
Move Over for Oklahoma Kid
Mickey's 565-Foot Drive
Recalls Ruth, Foxx Feats

Ruth and Foxx were baseball's long-distance elite up to that time, virtually adjectival when power was being described. Being slugged into the same headline as those boys was serious business and, from the normally conservative *Sporting News*, meaningful sanction.

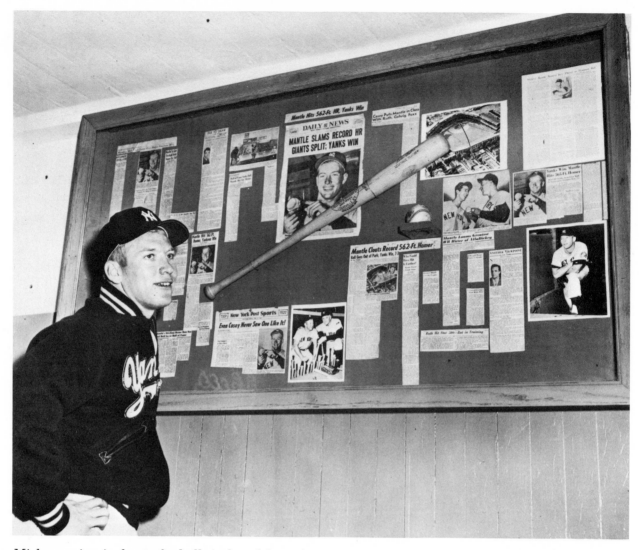

Mickey posing in front of a bulletin board featuring newspaper stories about the Griffith Stadium blast.

The story noted that in an exhibition game in Pittsburgh the week before, Mantle had become only the third man ever to hit one over the right-field roof in Forbes Field (Ruth, inevitably, was one of the three). And it was further noted that each of Mickey's drives had come from a different side of the plate. This dual power was what seemed to impress baseball people about the boy more than anything else.

If the Griffith Stadium home run remains one of the building blocks of the Mantle legend, the blow had short-term consequences that were ironic, for having been suddenly elevated into the Ruthian pantheon once more aroused those earlier expectations, and once

more Mickey was not ready to fulfill them, to the dismay and resentment of Yankees fans. When the man who had hit the 565-foot home run ended that 1953 season with 21 home runs, it just wasn't enough.

In 1954, Mantle batted .300 on the button and reached new personal highs with 27 home runs and 102 runs batted in. While the 27 home runs led the club, Berra drove in 125 runs, and Yogi and two other Yankees out-batted Mickey.

Mantle now had three full seasons behind him, very solid seasons, but still nowhere near the pageantry of slugging that had been forecast for him, and for which the fans were still waiting. He had yet to equal some of the stan-

In front, pitchers Allie Reynolds (left) and Vic
Raschi; behind, Yogi Berra (left) and Mantle.

Vic Raschi.

dards set by previous Yankees belters like
Charlie Keller, Tommy Henrich, Bill Dickey,
and George Selkirk, much less approach the
sublime heights routinely scaled by Ruth,
Gehrig, and DiMaggio.

But in 1954, Mantle was expected by Yankees fans to meet more immediate standards.
Through the years of Ruth, Gehrig, and
DiMaggio the greatest player in town had always been a Yankee, and as much pride was
taken in that as winning. Having a beyond-
the-limits player in the uniform of their team
always evokes tremendous pride in fans (as
Mets fans for years reveled in possessing Tom
Seaver, whose presence helped alleviate the
distress of years of indifferent teams). In 1954,
Mays was back with the Giants, rip-roaring
to an MVP season with a league-leading .345
batting average, 41 home runs, and 110 runs
batted in, in addition to his electrifying play
in center field. And in Brooklyn Snider batted

.341, hit 40 home runs, drove in 130 runs,
and, like Mays, played center field to its peak.

Mantle was not only expected to hit better
than anyone in New York (which to Yankees
fans meant better than anyone in baseball),
but also to provide leadership on the team
and inspiration for the customers, who for three
decades had been accustomed to seeing a genuine icon among the pinstripes. For Mantle
this was an unfair burden. Coming up unusually early to the major leagues, he "stayed
young a long time." The shy young man from
small-town Oklahoma simply was not ready
to provide intangible dynamism for baseball's
greatest team in the world's greatest city.
(According to one writer, Mantle lacked "ambition," which was as amorphous a charge as
could be imagined.)

There was something nicely ironic about
baseball's most corporate team always having a "leader," a chief executive officer out on

the field. (Ace pitcher Whitey Ford was later to be dubbed "The Chairman of the Board," in reference to the quality gap between Whitey and the rest of the staff.) This kind of chairmanship was never expected of Mays or Snider. Willie's ingenuous personality precluded it (in the early years anyway), and Snider was always surrounded by individual talents of considerable stature.

The residue of what many Yankees fans perceived as Mantle's failure to play up to those early expectations continued. In an article in *Sport* magazine in 1955, sportswriter Milton Gross described the reaction from a packed Yankee Stadium one night when the PA announcer intoned, *Batting third and playing center field, No. 7, Mickey Mantle—* ". . . the boos rolled across the huge ball park like thunder on a summer night."

To Gross, to the other writers, to Mantle's teammates, to the opposition, it was inexplicable. Next to Williams, Mickey was the most charismatic at bat in the league. He was the premier Yankee, on his way that season to his first home run title. No one, not even his most vociferous detractors, would question the tremendous effort he put out at the plate, on the bases, in the field.

"They don't boo him because he makes mistakes," Stengel said. "He doesn't make many mistakes. He does more things better than anybody else. But they slam him anyway. It's not right."

He was "puzzled," Mantle said, by the booing he received from the hometown fans (he was virtually never booed on the road). Not resentful, "puzzled." The uncomplicated youngster had still not fully adjusted to the sophis-

Part of the Yankees machine in 1953, the year the team took its fifth consecutive pennant and world championship (left to right)*: Yogi Berra, Mantle, Joe Collins, Hank Bauer, Gene Woodling.*

Ford and Mantle in 1954.

ticated and not-so-sophisticated complexities of the roiling metropolis. The press continued to predict his wondrous future, and it was from those very expectations, buttressed by statements from the Yankees, that much of the puzzling hostility derived. The press and the New York Yankees. Two very grand institutions. The fans had been informed, told, lectured: This was the coming man, the one who would make them forget the departed flagship in center field. And when the youngster did not immediately make those assurances ring true, that segment of paying customers who had an intuitive dislike and suspicion of grand institutions let their feelings be known. It was a chance to commit a bit of harmless anarchy by mocking and ridiculing these and all the other extravagant pronouncements from these and all the other grand institutions that had proved empty.

So Mantle's ascent to glory was more difficult than that of most of baseball's supernova. He wasn't just touted as a player to be compared with Ruth and DiMaggio; he was to replace DiMaggio while Joe's shoes were

still warm. That he did not immediately achieve this stature left him in disfavor with the disgruntled; that would take years to dispel, because there was nothing vivid or intriguing in his personality (for a city that placed a lot of store in these intangibles). He lacked the bubbly innocence and infectious congeniality of Mays. He did not have the cool dignity and almost mysterious persona of DiMaggio, nor did he have the poetry and flavorsome testiness of Williams, nor the endearing boisterousness of Ruth. Unlike Snider, he did not flare out and berate the naysayers. Though secure in his talent and in his relationship with his teammates, and having the total respect and admiration of the opposition, he projected no definable image to an image-conscious city. Where Gehrig and DiMaggio had been noble in their quiet modesty, Mantle seemed dull. When running to and from his position in center field, or working his home run trot around the bases, his head was always down. Cordial and amicable though he generally was with the press, he had little to say. He was there and not there,

The Mick

It was a solid season, but a year later Mickey made it look like small potatoes as he took his leap to greatness, and New York, the city that prided itself on having everything and having it to abundance, suddenly realized it had a third great center fielder, one to match and maybe even surpass Snider and Mays.

In 1956 the twenty-four-year-old Yankees slugger rolled through the baseball summer like a prodigious symphony, putting on one of the most awesome and sustained offensive shows in modern baseball history as he became only the fifth American League player ever to win the Triple Crown. The names of the previous winners—Cobb, Foxx, Gehrig, Williams (twice)—alone are enough to attest to the splendor of the achievement. Mantle did it with a .353 batting average, 52 home runs, and 130 runs batted in. He also swept honors in slugging, total bases, and runs scored. It all earned him the first of his three Most Valuable Player awards.

seemingly indifferent to the booing and unimpressed with himself.

But gradually, by hitting home runs farther and more often than anyone else, by being stoic under the stress of pain and injury, by allowing his own personal dignity to evolve in its own absorbing way, he slowly began to be appreciated, like some long-neglected or misunderstood work of art. And when the recognition and the esteem began to come to him, it never stopped; it kept expanding and growing, until in postretirement he became, after DiMaggio, the most glamorous of baseball players.

In 1955, Mantle led the American League with 37 home runs, batted .306, and drove across 99 runs. He also tied teammate Andy Carey for the lead in triples with 11, and in so doing became the first American League player ever to lead in those two seemingly incompatible categories, home runs and triples. He also topped the league in bases on balls and slugging average.

Mantle on the dugout steps at Yankee Stadium.

*The façade atop the right-field grandstand at Yankee Stadium that Mantle
came within inches of clearing.*

Early in the season, on May 30, Mantle keynoted his 1956 theme by racking up another explosive "spectacular" at home plate. It occurred at Yankee Stadium, a ball park that despite its inviting right-field target was built with dimensions so spacious it had—and to this date still has—contained the mightiest of sluggers. Not Ruth, not Gehrig, not Williams, not any of them, had ever come close to lifting a ball clear over the right-field roof and out of the stadium. The filigreed gray-green façade above the third tier of the grandstand remains baseball's unscaled peak. If Ruth, the most regal dynamo on the game's powerhouse scroll, the standard-setting Hercules, had never done it, then it must be impossible. But the feat was finally brought into the realm of the possible, by Mickey Mantle.

Batting against Washington's Pedro Ramos on that May 30, Mantle did not quite

Mickey Mantle.

Allie Reynolds.

send the ball over the roof, but he came tantalizingly close, the ball striking the façade and missing by an estimated eighteen inches of going clear out. It was the second of Mickey's landmark home runs, one to match his imagination-stirring 565-foot blast of three years earlier. The splendid baseball historian Robert Creamer wrote of the shot, "He came so close to making history that he made it."

Mickey's booming home run was hit in a context dramatically fitting. At the end of the game on that May 30, 1956, he had 20 home runs, a total that put him 12 games ahead of the pace set by Ruth when Babe established his record 60 in 1927. This was the standard stopwatch they held on aspirants to Ruth's record: At this point in the schedule, how many did the Babe have? Well, in all of baseball history, before 1956 and since 1956, no man

has ever had as many as 20 home runs at the end of May. This was going after a major slugging record with flair. To have people saying as early as the end of May that you were shooting for the game's most glamorous single-season record was to put appetite and anticipation at poise for a long time.

Well, he didn't make it, but in the process he hardly disgraced himself. In surpassing the half-century mark in home runs, Mantle joined another club known for its sublime exclusivity, one that not even Gehrig or Williams were part of. Only seven previous men had eclipsed the 50-home run mark: Babe Ruth (four times), Jimmie Foxx (twice), and Hank Greenberg in the American League, and Hack Wilson, Ralph Kiner (twice), Johnny Mize, and Willie Mays in the National.

By the close of the 1956 season, the second

coming of Joe DiMaggio had been forgotten; instead, Yankees fans were celebrating the arrival of Mickey Charles Mantle. Though still shy of his twenty-fifth birthday, he was playing his sixth season in the big leagues, the season in which he resoundingly put forever behind him the troublesome words "promise" and "potential," fulfilled all of the forecasts and silenced the last of the doubters, and joined the purest bloods of the sluggers' stable. The Mantle legend was now airborne and in permanent flight.

With their man having hammered through a season of such lusty proportions, Yankees fans were able to join New York's center field debate with not just loyalty but conviction. Snider had taken the National League home run crown with 43, driven in 101 runs, and batted .292. In the Polo Grounds, Mays had hit 36 home runs, driven in just 84 runs, and

Mantle and Stengel.

batted .296. The National League entry had done all right, holding its ground. It was the Yankee who had advanced spectacularly. He was unquestionably of their class now, and maybe even beyond.

He was a threat at any given moment to drive a ball five hundred feet or, with his startling speed afoot, beat out a routine ground ball to the infield (he was clocked at 3.1 from the batter's box to first base batting left-handed, 3.5 right-handed). Power and speed, baseball's twin generators. Seldom are they packaged together in one man; never were they present to such magnitude in a single man as they were in Mantle. Join him to New York, gloss him with a growing mystique all his own, and soon where he stands becomes hallowed ground.

Physical strength in a baseball player, unlike that of a football player, is not always readily apparent to the fan. To those who saw him undraped in the clubhouse, Mantle's brawn was impressive, from the thickness of his neck to the solid muscularity of his shoulders and arms to the muscles rippling through his back "like a heavyweight's." On the field its use was to the point of high refinement, bunching in flawless interaction to propel the sweep of the bat, all coordinates working in conjunction at the moment of contact, and then as the struck ball rose and soared in abrupt departure from the premises, only then was the immense strength and tense discipline controlling it bespoken.

White Sox manager Marty Marion, who played with Stan Musial, Johnny Mize, and Joe Medwick, described a Mantle home run: "He swung just as easy and *whup!* It was gone. Way up there. I never saw anything like it."

Nelson Fox, one of the scrappiest of second basemen, remembered the only times he was ever uncomfortable on a ball field. "It was when Mickey was on first and somebody hit a grounder and there was going to be a play at second and I was covering. You could hear him coming, and it got loud in a hurry because he ran so damned fast, so fast that it

Mickey beating out an infield hit at the Stadium in 1956. Covering the bag, Cleveland pitcher and future Yankees manager Bob Lemon.

Elston Howard, who replaced Yogi Berra behind the plate.

was almost impossible to make the pivot and get away from the bag. When he slid in and hit you—it was always clean, mind you—it was like nobody else. It was like getting plowed under by a Mack truck."

The impact he made on opposing players went beyond Al Kaline's "I wish I was half the ballplayer he is," and Harvey Kuenn's "His strength isn't human." You have to be, in the words of one writer, "a man-and-a-half" before other ballplayers will even begin to think you're any different or any better, and more than that before they begin carving pedestals for you.

With his running speed and batting power, ballplayers said Mantle did "the impossible." Mantle modified the existing circumstances, toppled barriers, expanded parameters, and established precedents. It was "impossible" to hit a ball fair out of Yankee Stadium; not only had it never been done, but nobody had even come close. Mantle came close; by missing by less than two feet he had compromised the

impossibility of doing it and cleared the cloud shroud from that particular peak.

As Mantle won more and more acceptance from Yankee Stadium crowds and all components of his physical ability became acknowledged and appreciated, increasing note was taken of his personality, of who he was. As his achievements became more and more explosive, what seemed to be a modest quality at the core—that shyness—began casting him in an engaging aura. Self-effacing he was as a rookie, self-effacing he remained as a Triple Crown winner and one of the most idolized and publicized men in America.

There was a likeable quality to many of the Mantle stories that circulated in his 1950s heyday. One of them was even reminiscent of Ruth's greeting to Marshal Ferdinand Foch when the Babe was introduced to France's World War I hero in New York: "I hear you were in the war." When Mickey was introduced to one of the twentieth century's most celebrated personalities, the vacuous Duke of Windsor, the duke said, "I've heard of you," to which a shyly smiling Mantle replied, "I've heard about you, too."

Clete Boyer, the Yankees classy third baseman.

To those who knew him and around whom he was comfortable, the young slugger from Commerce, Oklahoma, projected a different personality. In the clubhouse, at the batting cage, he was a warm and friendly man with a dry wit, adept at the rough-hewn give-and-take humor of athletes. He gave no indication that he regarded himself as special (although his teammates surely thought he was). A favorite story of his derived from the remark made to him by a teammate's young son who had been given the run of the locker room. After a particularly bad day in which he struck out three times in a tough Yankees loss, Mickey was sitting in front of his locker, gazing somberly at the floor. The little boy came by and tapped him on the shoulder. Mantle looked up, expecting to hear some words of encouragement. The boy looked at him and said, "You stink." For years it was a story Mickey relished telling on himself.

Like everything else about him, Mickey's temper was king-sized, and ballplayers enjoyed describing the eruptions. He kicked things and threw things and broke things, and seeing all of that immense physical

Mantle in 1960.

strength broken free from control amused his teammates. An emperor in fury left indelible impressions. Striking out once in Baltimore, he returned to the dugout in a rage and kicked over a ten-gallon container of water, turning the dugout floor into a running stream. But never, in these stories or in others told about him, was there a derogatory word spoken about Mantle, not by teammates, not by opponents. Sniping at big stars being common practice, this was highly unusual.

The affection his teammates had for him gradually grew to reverence. Like DiMaggio before him, he evoked these feelings without seeking them. DiMaggio's magic was alluring enough to attract loyalties despite a rather closed personality. Mantle was a more egalitarian type. He went out of his way to befriend, and the more his stature grew, the kinder and more sensitive he was to his teammates, especially rookies. When first-year man Tom Tresh was asked to make a midseason switch from shortstop to left field, he came into the clubhouse to find Mantle examining his, Tresh's, glove.

"It's too small for the outfield," Mickey said.

"It's the only one I have," Tresh said.

Mantle then gave Tresh a new glove he had almost finished breaking in. When Tresh sought to return it after the game, Mantle insisted he keep it.

"He did it quietly," Tresh said. "I don't even think anybody else knew about it. That's the way he was. If he wanted to do something for you, or ask you if you needed something, he always pulled you aside and did it quietly. That's the way he was."

Some people felt that Mantle's consideration for rookies was a reaction to the coolness he himself had received from DiMaggio in 1951, a coolness that may only have been a product of DiMaggio's natural reserve. By his own admission, Mickey was too scared to say more than hello to the man he describes as "a loner, always restrained, often secretive." It was quite different from being shy, and the boy from Oklahoma knew the difference, enough to be still wondering years later why the aging titan, surely not unaware of what was happening in that camp, did not suggest they sit down and talk. That DiMaggio generally ignored the sparkling youngster is surprising in light of his evaluation of Mantle as "the greatest rookie I've ever seen."

The romance of Mickey Mantle included a somber aura that was all its own. His father and two uncles had died in their early forties. It was said that Mickey feared a similar early demise (some writers ascribed the fury of his playing style to fatalism), and the plethora of broken bones, torn muscles, and other mishaps (including the osteomyelitis) that haunted his playing career did nothing to brighten this dark horizon. He evidently did not expect to attain a normal life span, to the extent that in one of his more celebrated post-retirement quips he said, "If I'd known I was going to live this long, I would have taken better care of myself when I was younger."

As much as his talent, Mantle's teammates spoke about his fortitude in the face of pain, the willingness with which he played with it,

Roger Maris, Willie Mays, and Mantle at the 1961 All-Star Game in San Francisco.

the stoicism with which he endured it. They knew that when he ran on those oft-injured legs it was like a man running along the very edge of a precipice; one misstep and he could be gone. And yet he never held back, putting out every ounce of his mesmerizing speed, be it coming out of the batter's box on an infield grounder or trying for near-impossible grabs in the outfield.

Sometimes his knee would buckle when one of his mighty rips did not connect, and he would have to hop and hobble to maintain his balance. "You can see it from the outfield," said Carl Yastrzemski, "the way the leg buckles under him and the way he winces with pain. Whenever I see it I wince, too. You can't help it. That's the way the ballplayers feel about Mantle."

He once said that he could tell when an injury was imminent. "I get tired and I start getting tight." Just before he pulled a muscle, he said, he could feel it tightening and getting sore. This would come about after weeks and weeks of his usual vigorous and uncompromising play, topped off by a few days of particularly irregular travel and inadequate rest. Then why, he was asked, didn't he avoid trouble by taking off a day or two? His answer went to the heart of what it was to be Mickey Mantle, to be any athlete of relentless competitive force. If you started easing out of the path of danger, he said, "first thing you know you're sitting them all out. It gets easier and easier to do it . . . I don't want to sit on the bench just because I'm tired." (This attitude is reminiscent of that of Pete Reiser, in so

Second baseman Bobby Richardson.

The injury was severe enough to sit Mickey down for the first two games of the Series, but he played in Game 3 and started in Game 4. In the fourth inning of the fourth game he delivered a base hit but had to leave the game when blood from the wound began soaking through his uniform. "He didn't want to come out, but I insisted," Manager Ralph Houk said. An ordinary man would have been home in bed to begin with. But not only was Mantle there, he played, which is cogent information about him, but even more so about the manager who penciled him into the lineup. Houk, like Stengel before him, was in awe of his star, up to and beyond the first drop of blood.

Ordinary players are not asked to play injured. But those of surpassing talent, a Reiser, a Mantle, those for whom the game seems to have been invented, possess a mystique so hypnotic it can numb the judgment and beguile the good sense of experienced managers who send their hurting stars out to play because those boys fascinate them, because the sight of all that talent simmering and compulsive is simply irresistible. Mantle saw nothing remarkable in playing hurt; it was not merely spirit or obligation; that mass of unique talent was its own propelling force and reason.

If Mantle was sometimes abrupt with autograph seekers and impetuous glad-handers, it was understandable. There is being big, and there is being big in New York. Two quite distinct definitions of big. There was also the dimension of being part of that special competition with Snider and Mays. Snider now had years of consistent excellence behind him, while Mays's leap to stardom can only be described as meteoric, to the point where he was already considered a candidate for all-time greatness. And now Mickey was of them, in equal partnership. And he had advantages. He was younger than Snider, and as far as Mays was concerned, well, Mickey was white. And Mickey could hit a ball farther than Duke or Willie, and he could run faster. And he was a Yankee, part of the Ruth-Gehrig-DiMaggio

many ways an early version of Mantle—a rookie sensation in spring training, center fielder, switch-hitter, unmatched running speed, injury-splattered career, and an esprit de corps exceeded only by kamikaze pilots. When Reiser was asked why he played while suffering from a severe concussion, risking fatal injury, he replied, "They didn't ask if I could; they asked if I wanted to. There was no way I could. But I *wanted* to. There's a big difference." Indeed. A great big difference, logical only to a Reiser or a Mantle, a foolishness so pure it makes itself sublime.)

Mantle's Yankees teammates became familiar with his performances under pain; they watched him sitting in front of his locker before a game patiently bandaging his legs (it could take twenty minutes or more). But not even these case-hardened teammates had ever seen anything comparable to Mickey in the 1961 World Series. An abscessed injury had caused a hole in Mickey's right thigh "the size of a golf ball," said third baseman Clete Boyer.

Maris (left) *and Mantle pose with former National League home run king Ralph Kiner during the 1961 season.*

lineage, which in baseball evoked the words heredity and dynasty.

For a player of Mantle's stature and celebrity, travel meant a virtual suspension of privacy. There were times when he was unable to leave his hotel room except to go to the ballpark. He would dine on room service, sitting and watching television. Sometimes he had to ask to have an incessantly ringing telephone turned off and the switchboard fill up message sheets for him. If he appeared in the lobby, the lounge, the restaurant, or tried to take a walk, he was quickly surrounded by autograph seekers, well-wishers, hand-shakers, back-slappers, and all the others who found themselves in the magnetic field of a charismatic baseball star. "He was a great guy to

be with," one teammate remembered. "A lot of fun to have a drink with or have dinner with—until he was discovered." Then it was like sitting on a park bench next to the man who starts feeding the pigeons.

A Yankees road secretary remembered the club checking into the Muehlebach Hotel in Kansas City at two o'clock in the morning and finding over one hundred people milling about the lobby. Stars like Yogi Berra, Whitey Ford, Bill Skowron, and Elston Howard filed through the lobby unbothered while the crowd surged toward Mantle.

"That wasn't unusual either," one of the Yankees beat writers said. "I'd say that was the norm. And it wasn't only in hotel lobbies and airports and provincial restaurants. I've

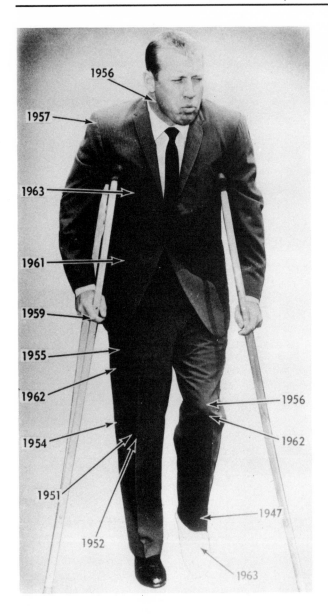

1956
1957
1963
1961
1959
1955
1962
1954
1951
1952
1956
1962
1947
1963

Mickey on crutches, with arrows and years indicating all his injuries. Here he's just broken a bone in his left foot leaping for a fly ball.

seen him sitting in some supposedly sophisticated places in New York where celebrities are common occurrences, only to be surrounded and fussed over. He could draw a crowd quicker than any athlete I've ever seen."

If winning the Triple Crown had meant vindication for Mantle and for all those who had been so brightly forecasting his future, it also laid upon Mickey a new and more difficult burden. This time it came not from the skeptical or disenchanted (there weren't any

of those anymore), but rather from his adulators. This ever-swelling chorus was proclaiming that now that he had entered his professional maturity he would keep getting better. Ruth, Gehrig, and DiMaggio, that haunting trio, had done it year in and year out, and now Mickey had proven himself of their class and would emulate them.

These new expectations that Mantle had to contend with were varied and demanding. Not only were his adherents expecting him to better or at least approximate his Triple Crown season, but he was also contending—in the eyes of highly competitive and baseball-conscious New York City anyway—with two players in another league, Snider and Mays. In addition, Yankees fans had become conditioned to winning pennants and World Series, and Mickey was the big hitter looked to to lead the team to further October glory.

The Yankees did win the pennant (though not the World Series) in 1957, and Mantle did improve his batting average, elevating to a career peak of .365, but he wasn't even close to the title. As if giving the young man a lecture on the presumptions of usurpation, the greatest hitter of them all, Ted Williams, at the age of thirty-nine, roared to an astounding .388. Nor did Mickey's 34 home runs and 94 runs batted in, each a highly respectable figure, earn him any titles. Instead of representing decreased production, however, those figures more accurately denoted decreased opportunity, for Mantle's problem was similar to that of a heavyweight champion who runs out of contenders: He was walked 146 times. Forgetting the 151 walks drawn in 1956 by the sharp-eyed Eddie Yost, who coaxed them out of reluctant pitchers, Mantle's 146 free passes were exceeded in American League history only by the two most feared sluggers of all time, Ruth and Williams. The pitching fraternity, with a survival instinct of feline acuity, had made a choice between valor and discretion when the young Oklahoman came to bat.

Protestations from Brooklyn to the con-

Full house at Yankee Stadium.

trary, New York's center-field laurels were carved up in Yankee Stadium and the Polo Grounds in 1957. Mays batted .333, far below Mickey's .365, but matched him with 35 home runs and drove in 97 runs, and was clearly Mickey's superior defensively. Willie, however, had over 100 more official times at bat than Mantle, giving Mickey a higher efficiency percentage. Mantle also outslugged Mays, .665 to .626. Snider, while outhomering the other two with 40 and closely shadowing them with 92 runs batted in, slipped to a .274 batting average.

But Mantle had no sooner solidified his place among New York's center-field greats than his two counterparts departed from the city. Snider with the Dodgers and Mays with the Giants set off with baseball's most unbelievable migration; the sun set on National League baseball in New York, and the big city belonged to Mickey alone.

Though the years immediately following the expansive feats of 1956 and 1957 were comparatively disappointing, Mantle was by now irretrievably among baseball's pantheon of elite bombers, recognized, applauded, and appreciated, all around the league but most especially in New York, where he had become the image of the New York Yankees, a most significant status since it made him a genuine heir of Ruth and a dominant figure in the world's greatest city, as part of its self-image as the Empire State Building. He was a most accessible symbol, too; you could take the subway up to the Bronx and buy a ticket and sit in the historic canyon with all of those championship pennants fluttering on the roof and dream of Ruth and Gehrig and DiMaggio and watch the current thunderbolt Mantle and go home and dream some more.

The Mantle legend had soared free of the earth's gravitational pull, to the extent that when Roger Maris, fellow Yankee though he was, ran Mickey neck-and-neck through the 1961 summer in pursuit of Ruth's 60—home run record, the hard-hitting Maris found himself cast in the role of unpopular pretender trying to seize unwarranted and unauthorized power. A certain segment of Yankees fans resented seeing the current embodiment of Yankees royalty challenged, even by one of their own. Maris, putting on the most exciting and glamorous season-long one-man power show in modern baseball history, was looked upon in some quarters as a usurper. Not only was he challenging Ruth, the most revered buster of them all, which offended older fans, but he was also outpacing the man now considered by young and old alike as the only acceptable heir apparent. The 1961 home run duel with Maris and the emotions it aroused was the most dramatic demonstration of the level of esteem Mantle had attained with Yankees fans.

More than Snider, more than Mays, Mantle came to radiate that common synonym for glamor and mass appeal known as charisma, that spellbinding quality implying inspirational abilities and achievements. New Yorkers do not often respond with such fullness; the city has seen, felt, and known too much. In New York's long three-team history, studded from 1903 through 1957 with 46 pennants, many remarkable players came and went. The glitter of statistics alone were no assurance of winning fervent, unambiguous devotion. The .400-hitting Bill Terry was not "charismatic," nor was even that citadel of high-power consistency Lou Gehrig. Mathewson was, and Ruth of course, and DiMaggio, and, for his own unique reasons, Jackie Robinson, and Mays. And Mickey Mantle.

Referring to charisma, a whimsical George Bernard Shaw wondered if "someday an intelligent bio-physicist will perhaps find out how to measure this force as we now measure electricity." In the case of Mantle, some tangible measurement was there—the 565-foot home run, not to mention the 3.1 sprint from the batter's box to first base. But that other measurement, the one that intrigued Shaw, of the quality that effused from the inner core of this overtly shy and quiet baseball player was not susceptible to scientific investigation; it reached into too many disparate corners for that, was too complex; for in the final analysis it is conferred more than it is proposed.

Throughout much of Mantle's Yankees years, Yogi Berra was generally acknowledged to be the most dangerous clutch hitter on the team, if not in the league. Someone once computed Berra's batting average from the seventh inning on at .430. But for one Yankees fan the man at the plate in critical late-inning situations had to be Mantle. When asked why, the fan replied simply, "It was *exciting*."

CHAPTER FOUR

If New Yorkers had manifested a rugged "show me" skepticism toward Mantle, their acceptance of Willie Mays was immediate, affectionate, and lasting. Mays had not received the overheated advance notices that Mantle had been burdened with, no figurative motorcycle escort or marching band to lead him into New York and up to the northern end of Manhattan Island, no noisy assurances that his career was merely an interlude before canonization at Cooperstown.

Giants fans went out to the Polo Grounds one day in late May 1951, and there he was, young, strong, sure, swift, roaming the center field of baseball's most bizarrely shaped ballpark. Ludicrous in its configurations though it was, the Polo Grounds' odd shape allowed one benefit—it gave Mays the most capacious tract in baseball in which to set sail and show off his defensive genius. Willie Mays and center field in the Polo Grounds were a fortuitous conjoining (as with an earlier Giants hero, the pull-hitting Mel Ott and the 257-foot right-field foul line). Putting Mays in a small park—

like Snider in Ebbets Field—would have been like trimming a masterpiece to fit a frame.

The fans could consider him their own discovery, without any undue prodding from the press. There had been no "man of the future" buildup, as with Snider; nor were there the expectations borne of spring training pyrotechnics, as had happened two months earlier with Mantle. Nor was there the pressure of replacing a DiMaggio, and of stepping into a lineup of a winning team that was expected to win again. Willie had been summoned to help a team that had stumbled coming out of the gate and that was floundering. Manager Leo Durocher and the Giants knew how good the rookie was, and so did the people in Minneapolis, where Willie was hitting an extravagant .477, to the extent that Giants owner Horace Stoneham felt constrained to run an ad of explanation and apology when Willie was called to New York.

Mays would have been a standout player and personality wherever he went, but being with the Giants enhanced him. The Yankees

The pride of Minneapolis, Willie Mays, in 1951.

had DiMaggio and three decades of astonishing success, and were in fact in 1951 in the midst of five consecutive World Championships. The 1951 Yankees had four future Hall of Famers (DiMaggio, Mantle, Mize, and Berra). The Yankees were in no need of a savior. If Mays had joined the Dodgers in 1951, he would have played left field and become part of baseball's most potent batting order, surrounded by the likes of Hodges, Furillo, Campanella, Robinson, Reese, and Snider (the latter four also destined for the Hall of Fame). The most interesting personality on the 1951 Giants was the club's manager, Leo Durocher. In May 1951, Willie was joining a team that had not won since 1937, a team that was, frankly, boring. A substantial number of New York baseball fans, those rooting for the Giants, had every reason to feel like poor cousins in the spring of 1951.

The arrival of Mays changed things in the Polo Grounds, almost overnight. Watching the remarkably gifted youngster race around the old ballpark's broad center field brought a sudden resurging joy and excitement that had been missing for decades. Willie's predecessor in center, Bobby Thomson (who was shifted to third base), was an outstanding fielder, but Willie was better. The rookie defied every struck ball not to be caught, whether it soared high and far, was scorched into the gaps, or was traveling on a low sizzling trajectory in front of him. Unlike the smooth Snider, who made it all look so easy, Mays's pell-mell style made it look daring, turning him into the most crowd-pleasing and theatrical man ever to play center field. He ran the bases with equal flourish, often running out from under his cap as he whirled from first to third on a base hit. It was a style of play Dodgers fans had become accustomed to seeing from Robinson; for Giants fans in the staid old Polo Grounds, it was a revelation, a wind tunnel of fresh air.

This most free-wheeling, exuberant, and uninhibited of baseball players grew up in a prohibiting and oppressive society. Willie

Mays soon after joining the Giants in 1951.

Howard Mays, Jr., was a child of the Deep South, born and raised in an environment of restrictive rules and ordinances framed especially for blacks, injunctions so ingrained they were seldom enforced because they were seldom broken. Despite having grown up in this hostile racial setting, Mays never evinced in later years any of the psychic scars of a Jackie Robinson or certain other black players. Willie's popularity, in fact, may have been furthered by this very absence of evident bitterness or suspicion or introversion; he was never a threat to the liberal conscience, nor did he ever demonstrate even a hint of the militancy that made Robinson so ominous a figure to so many.

Willie's talents and ingratiating personality were beyond question exciting and delightful, but perhaps they left him with an unlimned dimension. If Willie was the greatest ballplayer of his time (as many believe), then he was by definition the greatest black ballplayer. In spite of this, he did not draw

Leo Durocher pointing out some of the sights to the new man.

blacks to the ballpark the way Robinson did, and this probably went beyond the fact that Robinson was the first. More than just being a pioneer, Robinson was, by virtue of his seething pride, unforgiving resentments, his belligerency, and his outspokenness, always the symbol of racial progress and aspiration. For some blacks, the innocent, laughing young Mays seemed too close to the stereotype. Where Robinson threatened an accepted social order, Willie approximated a comfortable fit.

This is, of course, a matter of reactive personality. The injustices and humiliations endured by Mays were no less than those experienced by Robinson. Jackie was born to crusading and to opposing vigorously what was unjust. Willie's Birmingham ambience was foully oppressive, even dangerous. Robinson was raised in Los Angeles, where there was more tolerance, but no fewer slights and a lot more hypocrisy. Willie's response to racial prejudice was, "It won't change overnight. The old generation can't ever change. You have to wait for the young generation." Robinson refused to wait. He knew that change could be effected only if it was forced, if decent people were made to see what was wrong and what should be right.

Willie was born on May 6, 1931, in Westfield, Alabama, a suburb of Birmingham, the seat of Jefferson County in north central Alabama and the state's largest city. The South's leading iron and steel center, Birmingham and its environs were rich in natural resources, including iron, coal, limestone, and Willie Mays. As Mutt Mantle had been drawn to the lead mines of his corner of Oklahoma, so went Willie Mays, Sr., to the hot and noisy mills of his steel town, with the same wary regard for the mills as Mutt had had for the mines—once in, never out—and with the same parental credo: My son will have it better than I.

Like Ward Snider and Mutt Mantle, Willie Mays, Sr., loved baseball, played it well, and taught it to his son. Willie Sr. was good enough to play semipro ball and also with the Birmingham Black Barons of the Negro League. When young Willie found out that his father was being paid to play baseball it seemed to him "just about the nicest idea that anyone ever thought up—like getting paid for eating ice cream." (He himself, Mays said later, would have played ball for nothing; in fact, "I'd play ball even if they charged me.") When asked where he first started playing ball, Willie replied, "In the living room," meaning almost instantly, rolling a rubber ball from wall to wall and under and behind the furniture. Thinking of the boy Willie Mays rolling a ball across his living room floor is like contemplating the modest spring that is the origin of any great river.

When he was sixteen years old and still a sophomore in high school (where he was a star halfback on the football team), Willie was good enough to be playing with the Barons— professional baseball, in effect. One of his teammates was his father.

In June 1949, a Boston Braves scout named Bill Maughn saw the eighteen-year-old Mays playing for the Barons at Birmingham's Rickwood Field. (The Braves were one of the first clubs to show genuine interest in black players.) Maughn was sufficiently impressed to inquire about the youngster's availability. The scout learned that Willie was ineligible to sign a contract in organized ball because he was still in high school, not graduating until the following May.

Like Tom Greenwade and his high school

Shortstop Alvin Dark.

boy in Oklahoma, Bill Maughn did not forget. A year later he was back in Birmingham, tracking his man, who was now a high school graduate and free to sign a contract (and not just free but willing and eager, too; no fuss, no lawyers, no agents, no bickering or dickering; it was 1950 and Willie Mays was waiting to sign with the first team that asked him to). Accompanied by another Boston scout, Maughn watched Willie play a doubleheader. The other scout was not impressed and put the kibosh on the deal. Thus, the Braves lost Willie, and baseball was deprived of the spectacle of Willie Mays and Henry Aaron playing in the same outfield for the better part of two decades.

At about the same time, New York Giants scout Eddie Montague received a telephone call at his Jacksonville, Florida, home from the club's farm secretary, Jack Schwarz. Montague was instructed to go to Birmingham to scout the Barons first baseman, Alonzo Perry.

Eddie Montague became the man who in search of a candle discovered sunrise instead. He came to watch a first baseman, but it was the Birmingham center fielder who riveted his attention and stirred his dreams. Eddie Montague went to Birmingham and, in his own words, "My eyes almost popped out of my head during batting practice when I saw a young Negro boy swing the bat with great speed and power." Montague compared the boy's hand quickness to that of a young Joe Louis. After commenting on the boy's throwing, fielding, and running, Montague concluded that the unknown young Willie Mays

was ". . . the greatest ballplayer I had ever seen in my life."

It happens. It happened to Paul Krichell on the campus of Columbia University in New York City, to Cy Slapnicka in Van Meter, Iowa, to Tom Greenwade in Commerce, Oklahoma, and to Eddie Montague at Rickwood Field in Birmingham, Alabama. Persistence rewarded, faith honored.

The Giants authorized Montague to make a deal for Mays. Learning that Willie was not

Larry Jansen, the Giants sharp, curveballing right-hander.

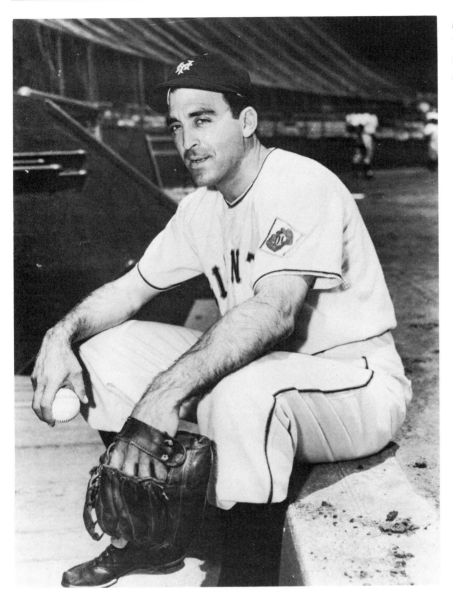

Sal Maglie: They called him "The Barber" because he gave the batters so many close shaves.

under contract to the Barons, Montague dealt with Willie's family, paying them five thousand dollars to get the young man's signature on a contract. Although they were not obligated to, the Giants also gave the owner of the Barons a check for ten thousand dollars to compensate them for the loss of Mays, describing the voluntary payment as a goodwill gesture (it also helped to insure them against any lawsuits the Barons might decide to bring).

Montague had signed Mays less than three days after first seeing him play. One reason for the haste was the scout's enthusiasm; a second reason involved seeing a Dodgers scout,

Ray Blades, in the stands. The Dodgers, in fact, had been tipped off about Willie the year before, when Jackie Robinson brought a barnstorming team to Alabama in the fall of 1949. Jackie had been impressed with the youngster, his only reservation being Willie's weakness in hitting the curve. The Dodgers, however, never made a move to sign Willie, nor did the Chicago White Sox, one of whose scouts had filed an adjective-studded report on him. A Yankees scout had also come and gone, noting only that Willie was weak on curve balls. (Closer to the truth, perhaps, was the fact that in those years the Yankees were weak

Three stalwarts of the 1951 New York Giants (left to right)*: Whitey Lockman, Bobby Thomson, Don Mueller.*

on signing blacks; otherwise shift the dream tandem from Mays-Aaron to Mays-Mantle.)

So, from the time he graduated high school on May 15 until the Giants signed him on June 20, Willie Mays had been available. But only the Giants—one of the few teams in the immediate vanguard of the Jackie Robinson revolution—offered him a contract. (How good was Willie at this point? Less than a year later he was dazzling them in the Polo Grounds.) If they had been preserved, the files of a number of big-league clubs might well contain negative reports on the ballplaying potential of Willie Howard Mays, Jr., which would be baseball's equivalent of Marcel

Proust's rejection slips and *Moby Dick*'s poor notices. Boston's Bill Maughn felt he understood the reason. "It was the color line," he said later, explaining how a ballplayer of such bristling talents could have been ignored. The clubs that had already signed blacks, Maughn theorized, felt they had enough for the time being (probably hoping that the rest would go away), while those that had not signed blacks simply were not interested in them. Another reason, according to Maughn, was that a lot of scouts were southerners, men whose ingrained prejudices were stronger than their appreciation for talent. At that time, four years after Robinson joined the Dodgers, only four of the sixteen major league teams had blacks on their rosters—the Dodgers, Giants, Indians, and Braves.

Willie joined the Trenton, New Jersey, club of the Class B Interstate League, taking over in center field. He played 81 games for Trenton, batting .353. He hit just four home runs, leading some observers to feel he was a line-drive hitter; but at the same time it was noted that the line drives flew over the infield like rifle shots, and with them Willie piled up 20 doubles and eight triples. Defensively, the new recruit rang up an eye-catching number—a league-leading 17 assists in little over half a season. The hustling young base runners of the Interstate League were the first to learn that something from a firing range had been slipped into the outfield of the national pastime. The base runners weren't the only ones wary of Willie's arm. "I never knew a peg could come in so fast from the outfield," one of the Trenton infielders said. "He could throw a ball two hundred feet and make your hand sting. His pegs came at you like pitches; right on the money and humming."

None of it went unnoticed. ("We had big-league ball in Trenton for a few months in 1950," one old New Jersey sportswriter recalled.) There was no question in the minds of the Giants management that it possessed a gem of many carats; so much so that when Willie went to Cuba that winter to play ball the club interceded and forbade it. They did not want to take a chance on having their young ticket to the future getting hurt on some lumpy Caribbean diamond. Willie had been hoping to pick up a bit of extra money, but all he got out of it was an extended Cuban vacation while he waited as the local team tried vainly to talk the Giants into changing their minds.

The Giants were so sure of Willie they ran him on an express elevator through the minor leagues, bypassing A and AA ball and assigning him to their top farm club, the Triple-A team at Minneapolis, then a major-league anteroom in the American Association.

Willie used Triple-A pitching purely for batting practice. After 35 games and 149 at bats into the 1951 season, he was hitting that almost indecent .477, and in the bargain exciting the fans with his defensive flourishes and winning their hearts with his ingratiating personality.

The Giants, meanwhile, expected to contend in 1951, had flown out of the starting gate like so many Wrong Way Corrigans, dropping down the well of an eleven-game losing streak almost as the season opened. So the Giants sent scout Hank DeBerry out to Minneapolis to have a look at Mays, to see if .477 really meant .477. DeBerry, a former major-league catcher, sent back a report that probably has no parallel in big-league annals, a report that was to remain valid for the better part of the next twenty years. "Sensational," DeBerry wrote, and went on from there with claims and assertions that would have embarrassed the most flagrant and shameless of Madison Avenue copywriters. "Is the outstanding player on the Minneapolis club and probably in all the minor leagues for that matter. . . . Hits all pitches and hits to all fields. Hits the ball where it is pitched as good as any player seen in many days. Everything he does is sensational. He has made the most spectacular catches. Runs and throws with the best of them. . . . When he starts somewhere, he means to get there, hell bent for election. Slides hard, plays hard. He is a sensation and just about as popular with locals as he can be—a real favorite. This player is the best prospect in America. It was a banner day for the Giants when this boy was signed!"

Reading this, the Giants had two choices: Give DeBerry a sobriety test, or call up Willie Mays. To the relief of the pitching fraternity of the American Association, they opted for the latter.

Aware of the esteem and affection in which the Minneapolis fans held their center fielder, and remarkably sensitive to their feelings, Horace Stoneham did a most unusual thing, taking note of these sensibilities in a paid

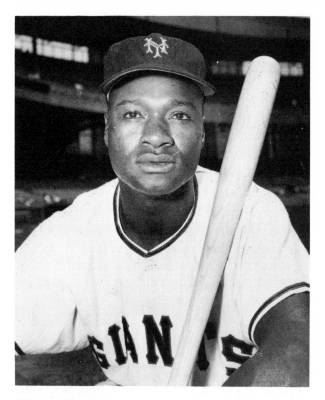

Henry Thompson.

Second baseman Eddie Stanky, one of the spark-plugs of the 1951 Giants.

statement in the *Minneapolis Sunday Tribune*:

We feel that Minneapolis fans, who have so enthusiastically supported the Minneapolis club, are entitled to an explanation for the player deal that on Friday transferred outfielder Willie Mays from the Millers to the New York Giants. We appreciate his worth to the Millers, but in all fairness, Mays himself must be a factor in these considerations. On the record of his performance since the American Association season started, Mays is entitled to his promotion and the chance to prove he can play major league baseball.

Willie and his .477 average were in Sioux City, Iowa, when the summons came from New York. When he arrived in the big city he went from the airport to the Polo Grounds for a meeting with Stoneham before going on to Philadelphia to join the team. The boss wanted a few quiet words with the anxiety-ridden youngster before casting him into the National League arenas. (Willie, awed by the thought of the big leagues, had asked for more

time in Minneapolis before going up.) A rarity among club owners, Stoneham, a baseball lifer who had inherited the club from his father, was unusually considerate and sentimental when it came to his players. He counseled Willie about some of the blunt realities of life at the top.

"Willie," Stoneham said, "they're going to try to find out about you fast up here. They're going to try you out with pitches at your cap."

"Mister Stoneham," Mays replied, "when I played in the Negro League, they threw at me too. Only it never counted."

"What do you mean?"

"They couldn't hit me."

"They throw harder up here," Stoneham warned.

"They can throw hard as they want. I won't be there."

For Stoneham, it was a cogent insight into the remarkable baseball perceptions and on-the-field self-assurance of Willie Mays. To the world at large, Willie was seen as naive and

*Brooklyn's Roy Campanella has just slapped the tag on a sliding Willie Mays.
The action took place at Ebbets Field in September 1951; Al Barlick is the umpire.*

simple (in the nonpejorative sense of the word); but when it came to the actualities of base-ball—that special, insular world all its own—he was as sophisticated a virtuoso as ever played the game, always aware of what he was doing, always knowing what he was talking about. The pitchers did indeed "try him out" with dusters and beanballs, but Willie, with his exquisite judgment and reflexes, was able to pick up the ball almost from the moment it left the pitcher's hand, and targeted though he might be, was seldom hurt by a pitched ball. Nor could he be intimidated; he was too quick and too tough for that. It was

as if those players of dominating ability—a Mays, a DiMaggio, a Williams—possessed an almost regal sense of self on a ball field that would not tolerate even the idea of intimidation.

Willie joined the team in Shibe Park, Philadelphia. Against the stunning pitching of Robin Roberts and a couple of other Phillies pitchers, he went hitless in twelve at bats. The rookie was hurt, embarrassed, and, after the third game, in tears. "You'd better talk to your boy," someone who had noted the distressed Willie quietly advised Durocher. Leo talked to him. The man whose name is as-

Warren Spahn, the most prolific left-handed winner in baseball history, and the man who served up Willie Mays's first major-league hit—a titanic Polo Grounds home run.

sociated with the words *loud, abrasive,* and *sarcastic* was able to sit with his arm around Willie's shoulders and talk to him soothingly and reassuringly. The gist of the conversation was this: You are my center fielder. Period.

In his next game, at the Polo Grounds, Leo's center fielder faced the estimable left-hander Warren Spahn, and the first time up Willie launched an awesomely struck home run over the left-field roof, a shot that left the Polo Grounds with such petrifying suddenness it moved Leo to this bit of poetry: "I never saw a fucking ball leave a fucking park so fucking fast in my fucking life." As the Giants fans stood and cheered, Willie sped around the bases. No leisurely home run trot for him. He always looked busy on a ball field. He projected New York hustle and bustle when he worked. He was an involved ballplayer, and

an involving one: People noticed, instinctively and naturally.

Willie won hearts quickly and permanently. Giants fans would not have been blamed for being skeptical at hearing about the arrival of another "can't-miss," franchise-reviving rookie. They had suffered through the recent failures of the clamorously heralded pitcher-outfielder Clint Hartung and the glitteringly introduced first baseman Tookie Gilbert. Willie, however, through the charm of his personality and the sparkle of day-in, day-out performance, quickly drew both respect and affection from press, fans, and teammates.

"I don't think any ballplayer ever related to the fans as quickly as Willie," Red Smith said. "Maybe Giants fans were more trusting, but they seemed to believe from the very beginning that he was the real article, that he had bypassed 'promise' and 'potential' and showed up in full arrival." A writer moving through the grandstands in search of a color story during Mays's first weeks with the Giants was startled to hear parents pointing out to the field during batting practice and saying to their children, "There he is. That's Willie."

They roomed him with the thirty-one-year-old Monte Irvin, a veteran, a serious-minded man of great personal dignity, whom the Giants felt would be a good influence on the high-spirited, unsophisticated rookie. Irvin remembered the young Mays as "a decent kid you'd want your brother or son to be like." Willie "was a fine young man, with a wonderful, happy-go-lucky disposition. No inhibitions. All he wanted to do was play ball." And consume large quantities of ice cream, pie à la mode, and soda pop. And then there was that other story that the Mays-infatuated New York press loved: Willie playing stickball with the kids on the streets of Harlem. What an image it projected! Could you imagine DiMaggio doing it, or Mantle, or Snider? But there was Willie, standing in the middle of a crowded Harlem street, between two rows of parked cars, broomstick cocked over his

Monte Irvin (left) *and Willie Mays.*

shoulder, ready to drive a rubber ball as far as it would go. It was the sort of thing that humanized and personalized him and left behind a lasting impression.

"He was a tonic to have around," Irvin said, "and not just for his great ability. Everybody was extremely fond of him."

People began coming at him in droves that summer of 1951, for autographs, for handshakes, for interviews, for business deals. There was already a sense about him, just weeks after his arrival, that he was somebody special and was going to remain so for a long, long time. Instead of trying to remember all of the names, he called everyone "Say, hey,"

which led to a lasting "Say Hey Kid" nickname.

Mays's skills and the team's response to both him and them are summed up in this story told by Irvin. "One day he made this unbelievable catch in Pittsburgh, off of Rocky Nelson. He was playing in close and Rocky got hold of one and drove it way out into that big center field they had in old Forbes Field. Willie whirled around and took off after it. At the last second he saw he couldn't get his glove across his body in time to make the catch, so he caught it in his bare hand. Leo was flabbergasted. We all were. Nobody had ever seen anything like it.

"Then Leo decided to have a little fun with Willie. He told us to give Mays the silent treatment when Willie came in after the inning. You know, you do that sometimes, after a guy had done something spectacular on the field and is expecting the big noisy reception when he comes in. So when Willie came back to the dugout nobody said a word. We just sat there with our arms folded and stared out at the field, ignoring him completely. Willie was puzzled. He sat there looking around waiting for somebody to say something. Finally he couldn't contain himself any longer.

" 'Leo,' he said, 'didn't you see what I just did out there?'

"Durocher didn't say anything.

" 'Leo,' Willie said. 'Didn't you see what I did?'

"Leo turned around and looked at him, poker-faced. 'No,' he said, 'I didn't see it. So you'll have to go out and do it again before I'll believe it.' "

Big-league baseball is a serious game, men will tell you, and no team was expected to be more serious in its pursuits than one run by Leo Durocher, to whom single-minded dedication to business was the track to success. But not even Durocher was immune to this gale-force arrival of fresh air. In fact Leo, as shrewd in the manipulation of talent as any man in the game, used to advantage not only all of Willie's physical abilities, but exploited as well the youngster's infectious personality. The skipper recognized Willie's bubbly enthusiasm as not only being integral to the young man's performance on the field, but as an asset to the club as a whole. Durocher cajoled, needled, pampered, and stroked his young star. Here was no ordinary talent, and Leo believed that a spirited Mays playing at the top of his game made better players of his teammates, instilling in them a pride of association, as Ruth and DiMaggio had done for their Yankees teammates in their own glory years.

It is unlikely that any move in the history of the New York Giants, short of their move

Giants owner Horace Stoneham (right) *and Mel Ott in 1946, two years before Ott was replaced by Durocher.*

to San Francisco, stunned and outraged the club's supporters as did the hiring in July 1948 of Brooklyn manager Leo Durocher to lead the Giants. Not only was Leo the manager of the hated Dodgers, but he was also abrasive enough to have transcended mere partisan passion and become despised in the Polo Grounds simply for being himself.

Why did the essentially conservative Stoneham so blatantly offend his clientele? Well, it had become painfully clear: His team was dull. His longtime manager and personal favorite, Mel Ott, was dull. Excitement for Giants fans had been the home run–hitting teams of the postwar years, headed by Johnny Mize, Walker Cooper, Willard Marshall, and Sid Gordon. In 1947 the team had hit a record 221 home runs, led in runs scored and slugging—and finished fourth. They had continued hitting home runs, and continued finishing out of the money.

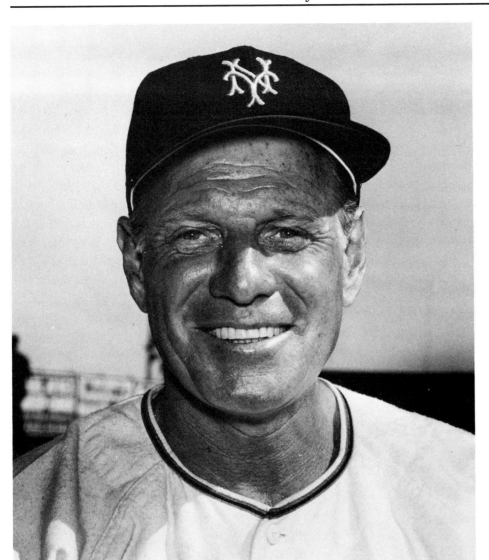

Leo Durocher.

This power-laden dullness might have gotten them by in a one-team city like Pittsburgh or Cincinnati. But this was New York. Across the river in the Bronx there was DiMaggio and the Yankees, and a long subway ride away in Brooklyn there was Jackie Robinson and a snazzy young Dodgers team emitting exciting danger signals.

So Leo came to the Polo Grounds in the middle of the 1948 season and soon began dispatching his dangerous but slow-legged sluggers and building his own team. By 1951, the Giants had cleared their roster of the big bangers, added shortstop Alvin Dark and second baseman Eddie Stanky, had solid men in Whitey Lockman, Don Mueller, Monte Irvin, Henry Thompson, and Wes Westrum, as well as a sound pitching staff. But the young player who had been expected to provide color and fireworks, outfielder Bobby Thomson, was having up-and-down seasons, coming to the brink of stardom and then receding. The Giants sluggish start that year seemed to doom the club to another unavailing summer's ramble through the schedule. It was into this Polo Grounds twilight that the most exciting, multitalented, and engaging baseball player of the postwar era was suddenly injected. Willie Mays was the man who came to the party and turned on the lights.

Durocher knew immediately what a spacious talent had been dropped into his lap, and he knew intuitively how to handle it. Mays was spared the sarcasm and the tongue-lashings Leo was so quick with and adept at. Willie was won over instantly. The skipper was "Mister Leo" to him; nor was this the subservience of a southern black youth; rather it was respect, tinged with, in the beginning at least, a certain measure of awe. Neither man had ever seen anything quite like the other. In background, personality, natural design, Leo was everything Willie wasn't. The Giants skipper was pure New York, a boulevardier of the sports world; a self-conscious fashion plate, quick-witted, egocentric, handy with his fists. He knew "everybody": politicians, entertainers, gamblers, movie stars, and other ornaments of New York's nocturnal world. He could be charming, witty, affable; and to complete the image, this epitome of the urban sharpie was married to a beautiful movie star (Laraine Day).

For the tough-minded Durocher, there was one primary touchstone by which to gauge the abilities of young ballplayers who would be great, and here again is the name of Pete Reiser, Duke Snider's predecessor, Mickey Mantle's spiritual precursor. When Reiser was a near-anonymous rookie setting afire Brooklyn's spring training camp in 1939, much as Mantle did in the 1951 Yankees camp, his manager was Leo Durocher, himself a rookie skipper that spring. Leo never forgot that sunburst of talent; it was as though he had been handed some sort of celestial good-luck gift as he was about to begin his long managerial career. So when Leo said of Mays in the spring of 1951, "I look at Willie and you know what I think of? Pete Reiser when he first came up," those who knew of Leo's reverence for the Reiser afterglow were impressed. There was no one in the league, Leo averred, with more power than Willie, or a stronger arm or better glove. And the skipper was speaking of a league that currently in-

Wes Westrum.

Monte Irvin.

cluded Ralph Kiner, Carl Furillo, and Duke Snider.

Durocher was, of course, a voluble cheerleader whose animated enthusiasms were capable of lifting manhole covers. A more meaningful recognition of Mays came from his teammates. As much as the Giants players acknowledged Willie's talents, they also took appreciative note of the young man's winning blend of personal ingenuousness and flawless professionalism. Willie's relaxed, carefree personality was contradicted by the emotional intensity he poured into his game. In the clubhouse he was a spirited youngster whose high-pitched giggle sounded his delight in the antics around him, while on the field he performed with instincts and perceptions that impressed his veteran teammates. The odd blend made him an athletic approximation of Kierkegaard's comment that to be

an artist is to have your life resemble a satire on your art.

These were the first demonstrations of the kind of talent that a decade later led another Giants manager, Bill Rigney, to emphasize a certain point when talking to a group of his young infielders in spring training. "When the ball is hit to the guy in center field," Rigney said, "get to a base, because that ball is going to come in where it's supposed to. Trust him. Willie knows." One of the infielders, perhaps curious, perhaps audacious, asked Rigney, "What does he know, skip?" The question caught the manager up short for a moment. He scratched his head. There was, he realized, no reasonable answer. "I don't know what he knows," Rigney finally said. "But Willie knows. So just get your ass to a base."

Willie knows, and his new teammates in 1951 saw immediately how much he knew. "We liked the way he played ball," infielder Henry Thompson said. "It was as simple as that. With the average player you take for granted what he's doing. You have a pretty good idea what he's going to do. But Willie was different. It isn't often that you *watch* another guy play ball. But you always watched Willie, because there was always the chance he was going to do something you'd never seen before."

Like the throw he made on Billy Cox. If the Mantle legend rests most prominently on home runs that seem to have traveled from sea to shining sea, then Mays's seems to spin upon an axis of stunning defensive plays. And not only diving catches and leaping catches and running catches, but throws too, and one in particular. How many outfielders do you know about who are in the lore and legend books for catches that defied geometry and gravity and who in addition hit 660 home runs, and are also remembered for a mighty peg that was whipped in from the outfield one August day in 1951?

"The Throw," as it has come to be called, took place at the Polo Grounds on August 15, with the Giants in the first strides of their

Ending the 1951 season in a dead heat, the Dodgers and Giants went into a three-game playoff to decide the pennant. The first game was at Ebbets Field, the starting pitchers the Dodgers Ralph Branca (left) *and the Giants Jim Hearn.*

improbable run for the pennant, which ended in that dream sequence known as Bobby Thomson's Home Run. The score was 1–1, the Dodgers were batting in the top of the eighth inning, Billy Cox was on third and Ralph Branca on first, and Carl Furillo was at bat. The right-handed-hitting Furillo sliced a catchable drive into right-center, in normal times good enough to score the run from third. But there were no longer normal times in the

Bobby Thomson.

outfields of the National League, now three months into the Age of Mays. Magazine writer Ray Robinson describes what happened:

Willie came over fast from left center and made a good glove-handed catch. Cox, meanwhile, had tagged up at third and headed home. But Cox never made it. And the 21,000 Polo Grounds fans who saw him fail, and Mays succeed, probably still can't believe it. As Willie grabbed the ball, running full speed, he stopped dead, planted his left foot and pivoted to his left. For an instant, his back was to center field. Then he was full around and unleashing the ball. It zoomed toward Whitey Lockman, the cut-off man at first base, and Lockman let it go through. When Cox arrived at home plate the ball—which catcher Wes Westrum had caught on the fly—was waiting.

Westrum later estimated that when it reached him, the ball had to be traveling at least eighty-five miles an hour, and that if an umpire had had to call it, it would have been a strike, "right over the heart of the plate."

"The Throw" helped win the game for the Giants and was destined to become a permanent part of the Mays Gallery of Great Moments; and as the Giants continued to accelerate their drive toward their unlikely pennant, it was looked upon as one of the drive's original generators.

Luck? Magic? A propitious conjunction of the planets? No. What Willie did out there was something much more fundamental. "When Willie was on the field," one teammate said, "he was absolutely intense. Nothing could

The jubilant New York Giants are surrounding Bobby Thomson after the big home run that gave the club the 1951 pennant.

Alvin Dark firing to first base to complete a double play against the Braves. Eddie Stanky is behind him; Sam Jethroe is the base runner.

distract him. You knew that for a fact because he was always a play or two ahead of the opposition on balls hit to the outfield." There were times when he seemed ahead of the batter, too. Some observers swore Willie was already in motion—unerringly—even as the batter was swinging. "He gets the signal from the infield," one coach said, "and so he knows what the pitch is going to be. He knows what kind of stuff the pitcher has, how the guy is throwing that day, what kind of control, and he knows the batter. He sees where the pitch is going and instinctively knows what the batter is going to do with it. You wonder why he's way back there to catch a long one and then how he can be coming in to take a line

drive off his shoe tops. That isn't luck. He's in the game pitch by pitch. God knows how many runs he's saved and how many games he's won just by *thinking*." Anticipation. Concentration. Sensing what the opposition is going to do, knowing his own capabilities for preventing them from doing it. Knowing. Willie knows.

Mays was "intensely proud of his ability," Monte Irvin said, though never "boastful or cocky." (And it is interesting to note how seldom a great ballplayer is boastful or cocky. When one comes along who is, like Dizzy Dean, it becomes a unique part of his lasting story.) And that pride runs like oil through the gears of the machinery of all great players, ready

Willie going up for one at Wrigley Field. The left fielder is Monte Irvin.

to respond at the slightest vibration. Once, a journeyman outfielder on the Pirates, Wally Westlake, passed Stan Musial on the field after a good round in the batting cage and said to the Cardinals star, "I feel great today. Like I was a lead-pipe cinch to go four for four. Ever get that feeling?" "Every day," said Musial.

Along with everything else he offered game after game, Willie was admired by his teammates for his fearlessness at home plate. He was a rookie, he was a dangerous hitter, he was black, and he played on a Leo Durocher team, all of which meant he was subject to a lot of sharpshooting from opposing mounds. (Much of it was in retaliation. Leo, always a willing accessory to possible manslaughter, was known to shout to his pitcher, "Stick it

*Willie taking his rips against the Yankees in the 1951 World Series. Yogi
Berra is the catcher.*

in his ear!") Willie's extraordinary quick re-
sponses to a pitched ball kept him from ac-
quiring dents in his head in those prehelmet
days; he hit the dirt, one writer put it, "as
violently as anybody," and then, "he's up in
a second and back over the plate, waving his
bat ominously and offering no word of com-
plaint. His teammates recognize that as the
mark of a real professional." That latter ob-
servation is an interesting insight into big-
league mores of the early 1950s. If a pitcher
targeted your noggin for a fastball, you were
expected to accept the assault with priestly
composure; it was "the mark of a real professional." A few decades later, the same pitch
is looked upon as an assassination attempt

and justification for a murderous dash to the
mound.

Willie continued to come to home plate with
an invisible target drawn on his cap, even
after the departure of the provocative Durocher. In the opinion of Bill Rigney, the most
flagrant threat to Willie's head was a certain
Cincinnati right-hander. "It was really aw-
ful," Rigney said. "Every time Willie went to
the plate against this guy the first pitch would
be right at his ear."

In order to try to combat the assaults upon
his center fielder (and center pole of his ball
club), Rigney let out word that he was plan-
ning a most novel form of retaliation. The
next time they played Cincinnati and the of-

*Willie scoring in the sixth game of the 1951 Series. Berra is the catcher, Alvin
Dark the next batter.*

fending pitcher came to bat, Rigney told a writer, "My pitcher is going out to play center field and I'm going to call my center fielder in to pitch. And I'm going to say, 'Okay, my boy, he's all yours. Here's the ball.' "

When word of Rigney's idea reached official ears it provoked a finger-shaking directive from the office of Commissioner Ford Frick forbidding such a tactic. It was a spoilsport reaction; it would have been interesting to see if National League pitchers would have continued potshotting Willie if they knew they were running the risk of stepping into the batter's box with the cannon-armed Mays standing on the mound.

So with their rookie center fielder hitting 20 home runs and batting .274, the Giants ran off their "miracle" in 1951. Willie was the on-deck batter when Bobby Thomson struck his eternally echoing home run against the Dodgers in the final playoff game. What Mays might have done if Thomson had gone out (it would have been the second out) is an intriguing bit of speculation. We do know, however, what Willie was thinking in the on-deck circle as that historic moment came to climax. "I was praying he'd hit it out so I didn't have to come up," he said. The 1951 season was so wondrous for Mays, as one writer later put it, that even his prayers were answered.

When he left to enter the army in May 1952, Mays had played in 155 major-league games,

The Giants knuckleballing relief pitcher Hoyt Wilhelm. He joined the team as a 28-year-old rookie in 1952 and pitched in the big leagues until 1972.

Don Mueller: He batted .342 to Willie's .345 in 1954.

the equivalent of just one full season; yet the impression he left behind was so striking that he was already being boosted into the same company as those two all-time center-field paragons, Tris Speaker and Joe DiMaggio. It was apparent to a lot of objective observers that if such canonization was decidedly premature, at least Willie *could* be that good, that he had as much or more raw ability than either Snider or Mantle. Though he may have lacked Snider's grace and Mantle's megaton power, he did have his own identity clip in his vivid individuality and in those tales of laughter. Snider seemed aloof and Mantle was shy; but Willie was the spontaneous youngster easily identified with.

After playing 34 games in 1952, Mays was drafted into the army and spent the next two years at Fort Eustis, Virginia, peeling pota-

toes, playing baseball, and watching Giants fortunes dwindle without him. (The team finished 4½ games behind the Dodgers in 1952 and in 1953 sank to fifth place and 35 games behind another winning Dodgers team.)

Because they came early in his long career, the two seasons Mays missed while in service

Willie saluting an officer as he leaves the processing center at Camp Kilmer, New Jersey, in May 1952.

have been generally overlooked as far as his lifetime totals are concerned. Also, because he had not yet blossomed into the prodigious star he was to become, the lost seasons do not provoke the tantalizing "what-ifs" that one associates with the interruptions in the careers of players like Bob Feller and Ted Williams, who went into service at apogeic moments. Since Willie hit 20 home runs in 121 games in his rookie year, it is not unreasonable to assume that over the next two seasons the rapidly improving youngster would have averaged 30 or more homers a year. At that rate, and it is being conservative, it would

have been Mays in 1972 and not Henry Aaron in 1974 who broke Babe Ruth's lifetime home run record. And in all likelihood, it would have been Willie's and not Stan Musial's lifetime National League hits record that the indefatigable Pete Rose finally shattered.

Willie was discharged from the army early in 1954. "Your pennant just walked in," a prescient sportswriter told Durocher the day Mays arrived at the Giants Phoenix spring camp. According to Leo, Willie was so eager to be back that he signed his contract without checking the salary figure. This was taken at

Willie in spring training with the Giants in Phoenix in 1954.

the time as another Mays anecdote, one that indicated his naiveté and his blind faith in the club. Faith there might have been, naiveté not necessarily. "Sure I signed without looking," Willie said later, and went on to explain that when you came out of the service, you always received the same salary as when you left. "I already knew what it was going to be," he said. "There was no point in looking."

As Mays went further and further into the 1954 season, steadily establishing the sumptuous range and depth of his abilities, the comparisons with Snider began. Certain things were agreed upon: Snider had more poise and style, Mays more spark and vibrance. Beyond that, there was little agreement on anything (these were, remember, Dodgers and Giants fans, historic antagonists occupying the same city, each with their own walled tabernacle, each rolling through their summer's rites, the most passionate jihad ever in American sports). Mays did the spectacular, said Giants fans. Snider didn't have to, came the rebuttal. Mays was exciting, said Giants fans. Only in comparison to the twenty-four dullards around him, came the rebuttal.

If there was a prime year for the Snider-Mays debate, it was 1954. Snider was steady and solid, Mays fresh and spectacular, the seeds he had planted in 1951 coming to full and luxuriant ripeness. In driving the Giants to the pennant, the twenty-three-year-old center fielder returned to the big leagues with a series of summer-long detonations. He batted a league-leading .345, hit 41 home runs, and drove in 110 runs. These were robust, man-sized figures, and that batting crown was not won without a certain flair, edging both

Snider and teammate Don Mueller for the title on the final day of the season. (According to some Giants players, Durocher's pro-Mays attitude was too overtly zealous in those final days, with Leo openly rooting for his favorite, to the resentment of some of the players, who had nothing against Willie but who felt such evident partisanship unseemly.)

Mays's defeat of Snider for the batting title on the last day of the 1954 season carried implications both significant and symbolic for Giants fans, for New York baseball fans. Both Mays and Snider put together highly impressive years (leaving Mantle in the shadows), and despite the fact that the Brooklyn

A familiar scene: Durocher cheering a Willie Mays home run.

The Polo Grounds during the 1951 World Series. The batter is Joe DiMaggio.

slugger bettered Willie in runs batted in, hits, doubles, and total bases, there were those—and not just Giants fans—who insisted that Mays had had the better year. Willie had the batting crown, the slugging crown, led the Duke (and the league) in triples, and had 57 strikeouts to Snider's league-high 96.

But there was no question that the two best ballplayers in New York in 1954 were the center fielders of the Dodgers and Giants. If Willie had the edge over Duke, and it was not unreasonable to think so, then this was a particular note of satisfaction for Giants fans, for only those with long memories could remember when the top man in town was a Giant.

One had to go a long way back, beyond Snider, Robinson, and then those Yankee behemoths DiMaggio, Gehrig, Ruth, maybe thirty-five or forty years, to find a New York Giant who was the premium man in town. The fine Mel Ott couldn't compete with the noise coming from Yankee Stadium, and even the brilliant Bill Terry and his .400 batting average had to contend with the fearful long-ball mayhem of Ruth and Gehrig.

He was "Willie the Wonder" and "The Amazing Mays," and with his bat, his glove, his arm, his speed, and his carbonated personality, he was sating the appetites of Giants fans. They were going to the Polo Grounds

*Willie has a bevy of beauties helping him celebrate "Willie Mays Day" at the
Polo Grounds in August 1954.*

"to see Willie," and that was sufficient unto
the day, because Willie *was* the Giants, the
most breathtaking diamond act in creation,
a brand new crown jewel in the city's studded
tiara. And if anyone dared forget it for a moment, there was baseball's snappiest exponent of the hortatory, Leo Durocher, to remind them. Leo had from the beginning been
the chief proslytizer, and despite his reputation as a dabbler in the hyperbolic, in this
instance the skipper found few who would dis-
agree with him.

(Occasionally the garrulous Leo would
overcook the selling of Willie Mays. One spring
training day in 1955, while engaging in a

game of pepper with pitchers Johnny Antonelli and Sal Maglie, Leo, feeling that Antonelli was not expending the proper zip for
the occasion, said, "More spirit, John. The kind
that Willie shows. Why, if it wasn't for Willie," Leo said to his 21-game-winning ace of
the year before, "you wouldn't have won ten
games last year." According to a reporter on
the spot, Antonelli turned around and walked
off the field.)

But Leo was to become part of a chorus. No
outfielder was to leave behind so many stories
of hard-to-believe sorcery. Everybody who saw
Mays play had a fireside story to tell, and
probably none more vivid than that told by

*Four Giants smiling after beating the Dodgers at Ebbets Field in July
1954 (left to right): Alvin Dark, Monte Irvin, Wes Westrum, Willie Mays.
That's Stan Musial in the picture on the wall.*

left fielder Leon Wagner (who played with
Willie in San Francisco). "The damndest catch
I've ever seen in my whole life," Wagner said.

They were playing the Cubs in Wrigley
Field, and Ernie Banks sent a vintage Ernie
Banks shot toward the ivy-covered wall in
left. Wagner ran to the wall, prepared to leap,
then decided there was no chance, that the
ball was about to become a souvenir. "And
then I hear footsteps. No kidding. I'm hearing
footsteps in the outfield and here comes Willie." It is a story not only of another bejeweled
Willie Mays moment in the outfield, but an

insight into Willie's full-speed judgment, daring, and concentration. He ran up to Wagner
"and leaped on me," said Leon. "His feet went
off my chest and he shot straight up in the
air and caught the ball. He caught that ball
and he didn't spike me. I still can't figure how
I didn't get cut. He ran right up me. Scared
me to death, man. Don't tell *me* about Willie
Mays."

It was plays like this that left behind a
Mays aura in the minds not only of fans but
of other players, who are ultimately the most
persuasive perpetuators of baseball myth-

Two great pitchers: the Giants Johnny Antonelli (left) *and the Phillies Robin Roberts.*

ology. "I told him," Wagner said, "I didn't know if he was good or if he was crazy." But it was more than good and less than crazy. What Wagner had experienced was the great athletes' appendage, something that refines the timing and the judgment and soars them to full and unique capacity: desire, a bizarre and incalculable kind of pride that sends them into the arena when they are in pain, makes them defy walls, makes them excel beyond expectations and establish elaborate new standards for all who know them and all who come after. For Willie Mays, there had been nothing remarkable about scaling the body of a teammate and using it as leverage to snare an airborne baseball.

According to Monte Irvin, Willie once said he felt that his greatest catch was a diving grab of a smoking, sinking line drive struck in Ebbets Field by Brooklyn's Bobby Morgan,

The two league batting champions showing their timber before the opening of the 1954 World Series at the Polo Grounds. On the left is Cleveland's Roberto Avila, who led the American League with a .341 batting average, and Willie Mays, who topped the national with .345.

which Mays took with a backhand swipe as he plunged headfirst at the base of the left-center-field wall. (This was in May 1952, just prior to Willie's departure for the service.)

No matter how myriad or varied were Willie's wonderworks, however, the catch for which he will be longest remembered (and probably the moment in his twenty-two-year career that will always epitomize him) was the one he made at the Polo Grounds against Cleveland's Vic Wertz in the opening game of the 1954 World Series.

It remains one of the most celebrated defensive plays in World Series history. Willie spun this particular bit of galloping wizardry not only in a World Series (the infallible way of having one's heroics memorialized), but at the game's most crucial moment.

It was the top of the eighth inning, the score was tied 2–2, and the first two Cleveland batters had reached base and were on first and second, with none out. At bat was the power-hitting Wertz, about to ride a tail wind into history; for as Tony Lazzeri had become to Grover Cleveland Alexander by striking out with the bases loaded in the seventh game of the 1926 World Series, so was Vic Wertz to become to Willie Mays: adjunct to a legend. All prior and subsequent visits to the plate, splendid seasons, entire careers, were to become so many sere leaves.

Wertz drove a high, simmering blast deep into that expansive tract known as center field in the Polo Grounds. Mays turned his back and ran, and ran, giving a classic demonstration of what makes outfield pageantry the most

*A couple of center fielders, past and present, meeting during the 1954 World
Series: Tris Speaker and Willie.*

enthralling of defensive plays. Willie's breathtaking artistry was in full view and full bloom for several seconds as he sped to outgallop Wertz's long, descending drive. When Wertz had tied into the pitch, there was probably only one man in the Polo Grounds who fully expected the ball to be caught. The pursuer, it seemed, was never in doubt. "I had it all the way," Willie said to left fielder Monte Irvin as they trotted in after the inning. And so he did. With his back to the plate, some 460 feet from the point of impact, Willie, heading straight for the bleacher wall, raised his hands over his left shoulder and made one of the stellar putouts in baseball history, preventing an extra-base hit, saving two runs

(at least) and probably the ball game (which the Giants won in extra innings).

Like an artist made uneasy by the emphasis placed on a minor work to the detriment of loftier achievements, Mays would always insist that the Wertz catch had not been that difficult. "A great catch," he said, "is when you don't think you're going to get there." He knew he would arrive in time for Wertz's shot. "All the time I was running," he said, "I had the picture in my head of where I'd be when I caught it, and how I'd turn to make the throw to second to keep the runner from going all the way around"—the films of the catch reflect exactly this, for they show Mays, a split second after taking the ball, whirling

The Wertz catch in the 1954 World Series.

Vic Wertz: Willie made him famous.

and firing it back to the infield with such velocity that after releasing it he spun around again and fell to the grass.

Years later Vic Wertz would say wryly to an interviewer, "Willie made me famous."

As has been mentioned earlier, up until the 1955 season, only six men had hit 50 or more home runs in a big-league season—Babe Ruth, Jimmie Foxx, and Hank Greenberg in the American League; Hack Wilson, Ralph Kiner, and Johnny Mize in the National. With the possible exception of Wilson, this was a list of elite power hitters, a list so exclusive that not even such titanic rocket launchers as Lou Gehrig and Ted Williams were included (nor were such later-day top-of-the-list belters as Hank Aaron, Frank Robinson, or Harmon Killebrew able to make it).

In 1955, the list was extended by one—Willie Mays and his 51 home runs. Along with his .319 batting average and 127 runs batted in (plus a league-leading 13 triples and 23 assists), Willie was now beyond question a member of the game's gilt-edged demigods, not just a player without a weakness, but one

Willie and Dusty Rhodes after the first game of the 1954 World Series, which Willie saved with his catch and Dusty won with a pinch home run in the bottom of the tenth inning.

of extraordinary strength in every category. With his flawless all-around play, comparisons with polestar center fielders DiMaggio and Speaker were no longer the partisan proclamations of Leo Durocher and Giants fans.

To some people, however, these opinions were still highly presumptuous (Willie, remember, had completed just three full major-league seasons). Predictably, the voices of dissent belonged mostly to the jealous guardians of the past. Rogers Hornsby, who always cast a dubious eye on modern players (nor was the tough old Texan ever going to be in the vanguard of the civil rights movement), said Willie would have to play at least ten years before

a definitive judgment could be made. Speaker himself, another Texan who would never be asked to address an N.A.A.C.P. gathering, agreed that the young man had a lot of ability, but also had "a lot to learn." But these amounted to sullen mutterings from the throne room at Valhalla. The more accepted opinion was that there was nothing for Willie to learn; it was all innate. One writer said, in unsurpassable summary, "Willie is a genius. What Einstein was in his field, Willie is in baseball."

With Mantle's Triple Crown season still a year away, 1955 was nevertheless the most lethal simultaneous outpouring by New York's

Another routine Willie Mays catch. This time it's in the 1955 All-Star Game in Milwaukee, and the man whose apparent home run he's intercepting is none other than Ted Williams.

three center fielders. Snider batted .309, hit 42 home runs, and led the National League with 136 runs batted in, while Mantle was winning his first home run title with 37, and batting .306.

Mays dropped off in all high-visibility categories in 1956, from 51 homers to 36, 127 RBIs to 84, a .319 batting average to .296. (Nevertheless, he still added a new category to his league titles—stolen bases, with 40, the first of four consecutive stolen-base titles he

would take. Willie remains, along with Chuck Klein, the only man in the lively ball era to lead the league at one time or another in both home runs and stolen bases.)

Some people attributed the decline in Willie's statistics in 1955 to the departure of Durocher (replaced by Bill Rigney that year) and Leo's subtle and not-so-subtle stroking of his favorite player. (Rigney had announced upon taking over that there would be "no favorites" on the club, an apparent reference to Mays,

Musial and Mays at the 1956 All-Star Game.

despite Rigney's being no less enamored of his star than Leo had been.) Nevertheless, there is little Mays could have done in 1956 that would have overshadowed Mantle. It was the year Mickey made the three-way debate one of equal persuasion. The Yankees star now had the statistics to glitter in the same firmament as Willie's batting title and 51 home runs, and Snider's 40-home run seasons and solid batting averages and runs batted in totals. If Mickey was not quite as luminous in the field as the other two, he nevertheless generated his own unique brand of excitement through his running speed and unmatched power. In the way of intangibles, it had become Snider's grace, Willie's personality, and Mantle's mystique.

In 1957, the final year of shared skies for the three great center fielders, Willie hit 35 home runs, drove in 97 runs, and batted .333, topping Mantle in homers and RBIs but falling far below Mickey's peak .365 batting average. Snider's farewell season in Brooklyn saw the Duke top his rivals with 40 home runs, equal them with 92 runs batted in, but drop to his lowest full-season batting average in Brooklyn with .274.

It was far too early in Mays's career for nostalgia to be gathering around him, but this is what began starting to happen in late July 1957, for on the nineteenth of the month Horace Stoneham announced that he would recommend to his board of directors that the club be moved "elsewhere." (Originally, it was reported, it was Stoneham's intention to move the team to Minneapolis.) On August 19, a

Willie at home after the 1957 season.

board vote made it official: The Giants, and Willie Mays, were playing their final season in New York.

So now the devotees of Giants baseball, and of New York baseball in general, were making their final visits and saying their last farewells to an old ballpark and a young player who had brought and was continuing to bring such buoyant resplendence to their game. With an ever-deepening sense of melancholia, they watched their man in center field, the days and the games dwindling to bottom in a vessel that would not be refilled.

"We never got up from our seats until Willie had disappeared into the center-field clubhouse," one old Giants fan remembered. "We

just sat there and watched him. Our way of paying homage, I guess. The last game of the season, they were playing Pittsburgh, and Dusty Rhodes made the last out on a grounder to short, and the Giants poured out of the dugout heading for the clubhouse. We watched Willie, of course, watched that number 24 race across the outfield grass before the fans could get to him and go up the steps into the clubhouse and that was it. It was over."

Gone into the clubhouse, the old Polo Grounds clubhouse of John McGraw (who once upon a time had his players punch a time clock when they came to work), the clubhouse of Christy Mathewson, Rube Marquard, Ross Youngs, Laughing Larry Doyle, and Frank

*Willie launching one of the four home runs he hit against the Braves
in Milwaukee on April 30, 1961.*

Frisch; of Bill Terry, Mel Ott, and Carl Hubbell. It was old and wooden, haunted by the passage of departed athletes, scarred with living spikemarks, redolent with the perspiration and liniment oils of decades past. But when Mays had roared into it with his high-spirited laughter and beguiling innocence, he was a refreshing gale whirling away the coarse tyrannies of McGraw, the dourness of Terry, the dull tranquilities of Ott. It was a palpable magic, at once contagious and animating. "It touched us all," Monte Irvin said. "You always knew when Willie was around. Love of life just flowed out of him."

Of Mays the veteran sportswriter Frank Graham had written, "There's no such thing as getting used to the guy."

The Polo Grounds.

CHAPTER FIVE

Shadows in Center Field

When New York's center-field triumverate was broken apart after the 1957 season, Mays and Mantle were each twenty-six years old, Snider thirty-one. Willie had fourteen years ahead of him in San Francisco, including some of his finest. For Duke Snider, the move to his native southern California was a moistening of his gunpowder. While waiting for a new ballpark to be built, the Dodgers played their home games in the Los Angeles Coliseum, an arena capable of adjusting to every possible sport, it seemed, except baseball. In order to accommodate the Dodgers, a ball field was laid out in the Coliseum that made the Polo Grounds look like a model of symmetry. Left field became a joke for its proximity, while right field, right center, and center were equally ludicrous for their extreme distances. With right center at 380 feet, and center field at 440 feet, Snider's power was nullified. In the four years the Dodgers played in the Coliseum, Snider hit just 68 home runs. (With right field virtually a blur on the horizon, the Dodgers began platooning

the man who had been their big home run banger.)

Remaining in New York, Mantle was now unchallenged for supremacy in the city, his star rising higher and higher until it found its place at last in the same galaxy as Ruth, Gehrig, and DiMaggio. Ironically, though he continued to be a prolific long-baller, Mantle, after 1957, had only one more year of true greatness—1961, when he paced Roger Maris to the home run record, hitting 54 homers, driving in 128 runs, and batting .317. There were some decent seasons after that, but the accumulated injuries had now begun a steady erosion of his talents.

Older they grew, their basepaths filling with shadow. They wheeled their bats with the same lustful intent, but contact was less frequent and fences seemed further away. Memory, selective and always seeking a manner of self-renewal, has fixed them in their zenith years, when each was so grand a player, so stirring to so many people, so ingrained in the daily life of a city. The seasons during which they labored through the cooling of their careers are like events that occurred in the dark and are little remembered.

Baseball history has been kinder to Mays and Mantle than to Snider, Willie's and Mickey's names climbing higher in the morning skies and brighter in the night. The big numbers, the thundering ones, finally enlarged the separation: Mays, 660 home runs, Mantle 536, Snider 407. The fact that in their New York years Snider matched the other two stroke for stroke was dimmed by the atrophic influence of the Los Angeles Coliseum on the Duke's career.

The vagaries of heated competition were also kinder to Mays and Mantle than to Snider. Despite his clutch hitting in pennant-deciding games (1949 and 1956), and his explosive home run displays in World Series play, Snider's career lacked the ultimate Great Moment which, in its capricious ways, baseball history appends flags and spangles to its chosen few and by which a man's full career is forever defined. Mantle has his 565-foot home run and the shot that almost flew out

Edwin Donald Snider of the Los Angeles Dodgers.

An overhead shot of the Los Angeles Coliseum. Note the right fielder: He's playing at normal depth, but notice how far beyond him the fence is. This configuration finished Snider as a home run hitter.

of Yankee Stadium. Mays has the Wertz catch, seen over and over on every baseball highlights film. Tellingly, Snider's most memorable at bat, the one most written about, is the single off of Robin Roberts in the final game of the 1950 season in which Cal Abrams was cut down at home plate—a big-money hit that was abruptly shortchanged.

Those long-ago debates on the streetcorners and in the bars of 1950s New York were seminars of illogic, bias, obstinacy, and an occasional cogent insight. If you had been there, you would have heard this:

Snider hits a lot of home runs because he plays in a small park.

What about the foul lines at the Polo Grounds?
What about the home runs Willie loses on those 460-foot fly balls to center?
Mantle has trouble with ground balls.
Snider should hit better because all he sees is righties.
Then Mantle should hit higher since he's a switch hitter.
Mays is a show-off.
Mantle strikes out too much.

And on and on, fervently, stubbornly, to no reasonable conclusion. You had the faith, and the faith dictated what you said.

During the height of the three-way rivalry, Mantle was asked about himself vis-à-vis Mays. "He's got me on three or four points,"

Snider with the New York Mets in 1963.

Mickey replied, and when asked which points, said with a smile, "All of them." But in his autobiography, Mantle takes note of both Mays and Snider. In praising Snider, Mantle points out the alleged props of the Duke's stature—the modest dimensions of Ebbets Field and the luxury of facing all that right-handed pitching. Mickey rates himself ahead of the Duke in running and throwing.

About Mays, Mantle writes that "Willie had everything," but that when he, Mickey, was playing at his best (meaning free of injury) he was as good as Willie. "Willie played at 100 percent all the time," Mickey notes, which is correct—from 1954 through 1966, Mays played in over 150 games per season (Mantle played 150 games in a season only four times in eighteen years).

Of the three, Mays was indeed the beneficiary of the most good fortune. True, Willie did lose two seasons to the army and played

his career in two of baseball's most peculiar parks—the misshapen Polo Grounds and the wind-ridden Candlestick Park. Nevertheless, he went through the bulk of his career without serious injury, enabling him to expend unimpaired efforts, squeezing every drop out of his abilities.

Duke Snider for five consecutive seasons hit 40 or more home runs, something neither Mays nor Mantle ever came close to doing. Two 40–home run seasons in a row was the best each could muster. In fact, in all of baseball history only Babe Ruth and Ralph Kiner accomplished the feat, Ruth the grand master doing it seven years running, Kiner five. But the Duke never hit 50, something Willie and Mickey each did twice. Willie won a batting title and two Most Valuable Player awards. Mantle has his Triple Crown and three Most Valuable Player awards.

Mays and Mantle rose to such heights of popularity that a permanent afterglow remains. Each, ultimately, seemed more "New York" than Snider, Willie with his *joie de vivre*, Mantle with his compelling speed and power. Snider played his Brooklyn years surrounded by a very elite complement, teammates like Campanella, Hodges, Reese, and Jackie Robinson, who siphoned off more pro and con emotion than any player who ever lived. It was impossible to become the cynosure on that club, as Mays and Mantle were on theirs.

Snider maintained and still maintains that the rivalry with Mays was something created and sustained by the fans and press. He and Willie, he said, were both professionals, and their primary goals were to win ball games, not engage in personal competition. Snider called it a "silly business," claiming that the writers were always trying to maneuver him into being negative about Willie. Mays as a direct rival, he insists, never entered his mind. Nevertheless, one has to assume that the somewhat introspective Snider was more aware of the Mays "boom" and his place in it than he was willing to admit. (Mantle was also part of the equation, of course, but Mickey was in the other league, looking at different pitching. Comparisons with Mickey lacked the immediacy and the aroused passions as did the comparisons with Mays.)

Though one must take Snider at his word, that he considered it a "silly business," in the light of subsequent baseball history, which has recorded Mays and Mantle as two of the greatest of all players, the old comparisons are flattering to Snider; at the time the abilities of the three were being debated there was legitimate reason to regard him as an equal of the other two.

The move to Los Angeles fractured Snider's career in the middle and left the Duke with a number of unfulfilled prime years, years in which he could surely have lifted his home run total to well over 500.

Unquestionably, it was Mantle whose career leaves the most to "what-if" speculation. Between time lost and games played with pain and injury that would have disabled a lesser man, Mantle's overall record suffered considerably. That the record is as impressive as it is makes one think wistfully about what it might have looked like had Mickey not been forced to play under so many handicaps. Certain baseball romantics have woven in fantasy the full careers of an uninjured Smoky Joe Wood, Pete Reiser, Herb Score, and Dizzy Dean; with computers they have tried to reconstruct the lost years of Ted Williams and Bob Feller. In the unique, statistic-drenched universe that is baseball, this is acceptable reverie, adding illusion to make reality more palatable. While the incursions upon Mantle's career are not as glaring, it still is not unreasonable to speculate on the grandeur of Mickey's page in the record book if his eighteen years had been free of injury.

So Mickey was the one who remained in New York, playing on and on, right through and then past his prime and into slow and very evident decline; at the end not even a center fielder anymore but a first baseman,

Mickey in the spring of 1969, hanging up No. 7 for the last time.

where he looked so out of place (as awkwardly dislocated as Snider looked with "Los Angeles" lettered across his uniform blouse and Mays with "San Francisco" across his). In his final two seasons, Yankees first baseman Mickey Mantle batted .245 and .237, respectively. He was playing because the Yankees wanted him to and because his hundred-thousand-dollar salary was too attractive to turn down.

Ironically, the star who had symbolized Yankees dominance, now, in his professional infirmity, came to embody the quietus of a dynasty. The Yankees stopped winning pennants in 1964, whereupon they took an abrupt and headlong dive into the danker regions of the American League standings. Mickey played on until 1968, retiring officially in the spring of 1969. Most of the players who had rushed with him across American League finish lines had preceded him in departure, traded or retired: Yogi Berra, Whitey Ford, Elston Howard, Roger Maris, Bill Skowron, Bobby Richardson, Tony Kubek.

Mickey Mantle Day at Yankee Stadium, June 8, 1969.

The bat was no longer quick, the legs were aching and heavy; but the legend was still robust, because despite the anemic batting average, he still drew over 100 walks in each of his last two seasons, because there was still a residue of the old fearsome dynamite left in the bat (those aging sluggers are like unexploded land mines waiting to be pressured by the unsuspecting), and because the men on the mound now had been teenagers who grew up hearing about the frightening power and had come into the league wary and respectful.

Mantle stayed, and the other two returned, came back to New York for curtain calls, spent, but wonderfully nostalgic. There was a new team in town, the New York Mets, managed by an old glory figure himself, Casey Stengel, playing temporarily in a resurrected Polo Grounds.

Released by the Dodgers just before the start of the 1963 season, the thirty-seven-year-old Snider was signed by the Mets, as a gesture to New York sentiment and to bring some of the old aura to a hopelessly inept last-place team. The Duke played in 129 games, batted .243, and hit 14 home runs, among them the 400th of his career. For Snider it was strictly a holding action, fingertip time for a once-great star trying to fend off the weight of the years. He played his home games in a foredoomed ballpark waiting to be demolished, a park that had once contained those fervent battles with the New York Giants of Willie Mays.

Willie Mays of the San Francisco Giants.

A year later Snider finished his career, ironically, as a teammate of Willie's in San Francisco, watching his onetime rival, who was still at his summit, crash 47 home runs. Snider got into 91 games with the Giants, many of them as a pinch-hitter, batting .210 and hitting the last four of his 407 home runs. And then it was over.

Mays, with more resilience than the other two, had his last productive season in 1971, batting .271 and hitting 18 home runs, and, significantly, playing 48 games at first base.

And, as the aging Mantle had, Willie, in his own decline, was facing those same young pitchers who had come of age awash in the legend of Willie Mays and showed the forty-year-old man the same respect Mickey had received—walking him 112 times, the only time Willie ever received more than 82 walks in a season and the only time he ever led the league in that category. (This in a season when Mays also set another personal high by striking out 123 times.)

Living legends can become cumbersome bits

Willie returning to New York in June 1962 to play the Mets at the Polo Grounds.

of luggage. The following May, when the Giants felt they could no longer afford Willie's salary (estimated at $150,000), and it was obvious he was no longer earning it, they sent him back to where a lot of people felt he belonged all the time—to New York, where a sentimental Mets ownership wanted the pride of possessing Willie Mays, though this was now a Willie Mays with much too much mileage on him.

So, a decade after Snider had returned to New York, back came Mays, five days after his forty-first birthday, back to a thunderous reception from those fans who had never forgotten, who had made visits by the Mays-led San Francisco Giants sellouts.

Willie with the Mets in 1973.

But the magic was all in the name and the memories now, for this was a man carrying the burdens of middle age, who had sore knees, whose bat could no longer get around on fastballs, whose legs had lost their speed. Center field was no longer his private preserve; the man who had set the standards now had to watch others try to attain them. He played in 88 games (only 63 in the outfield), batted .250, and hit eight home runs.

He would play another year, 1973, and there was no one to tell him not to. But this time the Mets found themselves contending for a division title, and a forty-two-year-old center fielder who could no longer play center field was a liability. Mets pitchers muttered about balls that should have been caught, while other players on the club questioned playing a man who hit just .211 with only six home runs and who was striking out better than one quarter of the time. But legends live on, even if only in their own shadows, and no one had the temerity to tell the frayed old emperor to move aside.

Then, just before the season ended, with the club locked in a sizzling race for the division

Old Timers Day at Shea Stadium. Walking in from center field (left to right): *Duke Snider, Joe DiMaggio, Willie Mays, Mickey Mantle.*

title, Willie formally announced that this would be his last year. On Willie Mays Night at Shea Stadium, he bade his imminent farewell, tearfully saying, "Willie, say goodbye to America."

The Mets won the division and the pennant and went into the World Series against Oakland. Manager Yogi Berra started Willie in center field in the opening game. Apparently the skipper did not like what he saw, and the next day Willie was on the bench. In the bottom of the ninth, with the Mets up 6–4, Willie went to center as the result of some personnel shuffling. He lost a fly ball in the sun, opening the door to a game-tying two-run Oakland rally. But in the top of the twelfth inning, he delivered a clutch two-out single that drove in the go-ahead run and led to three more runs that won the game. It was the last ray of the setting sun of Willie Mays. Except for one pinch-hitting role, he spent the rest of the Series on the bench, watching the Mets lose in seven games.

"Willie Mays on the bench for the seventh game of the World Series?" one writer said later. "That tells you something."

It told everything.

Nine years after the retirement of Snider, five years after the retirement of Mantle, Willie Mays, humbled by the encroachments of time, was through.

Their careers are long over now, fixed in the moving currents, statistics immutably engraved, polished plaques on the walls of Cooperstown.

Once, and simultaneously, they were center field in New York, young men at the ready in that most commanding of positions, charged with the mandate to "take whatever you can get." Center fielder. The most far-ranging of baseball players. And how far these three ranged, how surely, how swiftly. Rarely comes so equipped a ballplayer as these three were. And for several years all in unison. It happened, once upon a time in New York City, in Ebbets Field, Yankee Stadium, and the Polo Grounds, in Brooklyn, the Bronx, and Manhattan, in years long since spent, when the days seemed brighter and the nights more peaceful, and the clock seemed to move not at all.

Index